The
Complete
COUNTDOWN
Companion.

The
Complete
COUNTDOWN
Companion

Peter Newby
and
John Meade

PELHAM BOOKS
Stephen Greene Press

PELHAM BOOKS/Stephen Greene Press

Published by the Penguin Group
27 Wrights Lane, London W8 5TZ, England
Viking Penguin Inc., 40 West 23rd Street, New York, New York 10010, USA
The Stephen Greene Press Inc., 15 Muzzey Street, Lexington,
Massachusetts 02173, USA

Penguin Books Australia Ltd, Ringwood, Victoria, Australia
Penguin Books Canada Ltd, 2801 John Street, Markham, Ontario,
Canada L3R 1B4
Penguin Books (NZ) Ltd, 182–190 Wairau Road, Auckland 10, New Zealand

Penguin Books Ltd, Registered Offices: Harmondsworth, Middlesex, England

First published 1990

Typeset in Linotron 10 on 12pt Novarese Book by
Goodfellow & Egan (Phototypesetting) Ltd, Cambridge.

Made and printed in Great Britain by Richard Clay Ltd, Bungay, Suffolk.

A CIP catalogue record for this book is available from the British Library.

ISBN 0 7207 1935 6

Contents

Note: Answers, where necessary, are given at the end
of each chapter.

Preface

When the idea of *The Complete Countdown Companion* was first mooted I readily agreed, but my initial enthusiasm soon diminished when I realized the enormity of the task. I needed help and as far as I was concerned there was only one man in my book who fitted the bill – Peter Newby.

I first met him when he brought a coach-load of Scrabble® players from Derbyshire and Nottinghamshire to attend the first *Countdown* final. Such was their enthusiasm that I ended up paying for the coaches to transport them to Leeds for subsequent finals. At that time I didn't realize he was one of the top word specialists in the world and the father of two famous sons!

Peter responded to my invitation with alacrity. Without him I can truthfully say this book would not have been published. For my contributions I've had to rely on memory, aided by video recordings and game logs. Peter has had to cope with his brilliance and painstaking research. His work has taught me a great deal. I'm sure you'll find it equally beneficial. If my scribblings provide a little light relief on the way, then we've both succeeded in our tasks.

John B Meade
Leeds 1989

Foreword

Like all good ideas, that for *Countdown* was immensely simple. Choose nine letters – then try to make a long word. Or with the numbers game – choose your numbers, set a target and get cracking.

That was the basic plan hatched up by French TV producer Armand Jammot 20 years ago. His programme has been running six nights a week on Antenne 2 network ever since.

When we transferred the game to Channel Four, we adapted it slightly. We wanted to give more emphasis to passing time – so the clock, and its attendant music, became a major feature of the set. And, unlike the French game, we wanted to have a beginning, a middle and an end to each edition. So the idea of the Conundrum was hatched – the sudden death round, which in so many cases is the crucial round in which the winner of the Conundrum wins the game.

So, after eight years, *Countdown* goes on. It's a must for millions of viewers every week. People plan their whole afternoon round the 4.30 show . . . a cup of tea and a helping of *Countdown* make the ideal recipe for compulsive viewing. The advent of the video means that not only can people who are out at work watch it . . . they can also slow the clock down from its relentless pace to give themselves a better chance!

This book reflects the great interest in *Countdown*. The programme has kindled an interest in words, their meaning and definition.

I hope you enjoy this companion and that, of course, you will continue to join us all on Channel Four.

Richard Whiteley, October 1989

11

The Countdown to Countdown

Countdown, as a word, was first termed in the late 1920s, intriguingly enough, by someone in the entertainment business. Motion picture director Fritz Lang, whose favourite consonant was 'M', the title of his silent film classic, launched one of the earliest science fiction movies, *The Lady in the Moon*, the highlight of which was the launching of a rocket. Lang thought that the suspense would be heightened by changing from the conventional 'one-two-three' to exactly the reverse.

Countdown, as a television game show, had a much more complicated launch. The date was February 1982; the location, Yorkshire Television's Leeds studios. At that time I was working in the news and current affairs department, producing the regional nightly news and magazine programme (presented by Richard Whiteley), and various departmental off-shoots plus documentaries. All serious stuff!

The Head of Department was Frank Smith, former Editor of *Panorama*, who spent all his holidays in France. It was there that he first set eyes on *Countdown*'s antecedent – *Des Chiffres Et Des Lettres*. Frank, who spoke fluent French (I have to use the past tense, I'm afraid, as he died four years ago) was captivated by the show and brought a recording back to England. Enter John Meade!

Some years previously I'd produced a very popular series called *The Indoor League*, hosted by the former Yorkshire and England cricketer Fred Trueman. This series, which gathered together the best exponents of indoor sports – darts, pool, arm wrestling, bar billiards, skittles, etc. – was deemed by Frank to qualify me to adapt

Des Chiffres Et Des Lettres into an acceptable English programme.

When I first viewed a recording of the French show with my director, David St. David Smith, I was not too impressed and neither was he. It wasn't that our French was so bad that we couldn't understand it. We both just felt that it wouldn't adapt to suit the English audience and we duly passed on our misgivings to Frank.

Frank, the Francophile, wasn't to be so easily deterred, and he suggested that we fly to Paris to meet the producers and watch the show being made. Still David and I demurred until by chance we discovered that Wales was due to play rugby in Paris in the near future. A deal was struck. If Frank could get some tickets for the international, we would gladly go to Paris with him.

Two weeks later we found ourselves in a tiny Parisian studio watching *Des Chiffres Et Des Lettres* being churned out at a remarkable rate of knots and, lo and behold, David and I began to play along with the game. Whilst not being hooked we were certainly tempted by the bait.

So it was that on a lovely spring lunch-time in Paris Frank Smith and Marcel Stellman, acting on behalf of the French owner of *Des Chiffres Et Des Lettres* Armand Jammot, struck a deal.

It was decided that we would transmit six shows, based on *Des Chiffres Et Des Lettres*, in the Yorkshire Television region only, and then gauge the audience-reaction. But first we felt that radical changes would have to be made to the show, without straying too far from the original idea, for it to be acceptable to an English-speaking audience. (Marcel Stellman, who incidentally penned the lyrics to *Tulips of Amsterdam*, was appointed to look after Armand Jammot's interest. I'm glad to say he still does.)

First the name of the show – we were all agreed that the English translation of *Des Chiffres Et Des Lettres* (Numbers and Letters) would hardly pull the viewers in. After another bottle of *vin blanc* Frank thought that the centrepiece of the set should be a clock which counted down from a pre-timed target. (During the French game there was no clock – each round lasted a minute, to the accompaniment of barely discernible Muzak.) It didn't take long to decide on the title *Countdown*.

Who should present it? Well, as it was going to be a regional show to start with, why not choose the region's senior frontman? Enter Richard Whiteley.

We then agreed that Richard should be accompanied by an erudite celebrity to adjudicate. Let's fix up lunch with Ted Moult and see what he thinks! And so we flew back to Leeds, depressed that France had beaten Wales at rugby but confident that we had a potential winner with *Countdown*.

That summer we recorded *Calendar Countdown* with Richard Whiteley in the chair and Ted Moult in charge of the dictionary. In those early days contestants selected just eight letters and I had decided that we would have fewer rather than an equal quota of the numbers game as they still do in France, acting on my lofty assumption that the British are less numerate than our trans-Channel counterparts. (In those early months I was proved correct.) Oh, and by the way, the *Countdown* Conundrum was an anagram! More of that later.

Looking at those old recordings makes me shudder. Ted Moult and I discovered that leafing through a dictionary was not a mindless task but an absolute art form. He didn't have an adjudicator by his side, although I did have a member of lexicographers from the Department of English at Leeds University with me in the control room. The 45 seconds we gave to the contestants seemed an age. The vital statistician I first selected had marvellous qual-ifications on paper but she proved that paper cuts up easily: in six shows she didn't get one numbers game correct that the contestants couldn't easily work out, and, I'm afraid, in those days neither I nor my production team were mentally equipped to help her.

Still, we muddled through and recorded the six shows in the scheduled time, and we gained some encouragement from the enthusiasm of the studio audience. But what about the television audience?

Marcel Stellman and his delightful wife Jeanne attended the first day's recording and afterwards were publicly full of praise. It was only some years later that they admitted that they were very depressed on the journey back to London that night.

However, they were not depressed a few weeks later. *Calendar Countdown* proved an enormous success, going out at 6.30 on Monday evenings.

Armed with the viewing figures and a cassette, Frank visited the Commissioning Editor for Light Entertainment at Channel 4, Cecil Korer. After some agreement Yorkshire Television was commissioned to make fifty *Countdowns* to be transmitted five days a week – the first game show to be 'stripped' in such a fashion. Later we were told that it would be the first programme to be transmitted on the new station. Good news indeed, but changes had to be made. I felt 45 seconds was too long. Playing along with the contestants during the local series, I felt that if one didn't spot *the* word in 30 seconds then, under studio pressure, another 15 seconds wouldn't help them that much.

The time saved by reducing the countdown to 30 seconds could prove valuable, not to introduce more rounds, but to reduce the frantic pace that was evident in the regional transmissions. It seemed to me pointless to introduce a pleasant parlour game into the country's homes only for the viewer to end up breathless!

To enable players to come up with longer words we decided to extend the selection by one, making it nine letters. The final anagram would also contain nine letters, so we decided to call it the *Countdown* Conundrum.

In the early days of *Countdown* on Channel 4 I received thousands of letters from viewers saying the Conundrum was really an anagram. I replied, defensively, that an anagram was a transposition of letters from a word or phrase to make another word or phrase. As *Countdown*'s final nine letters were already jumbled up and could only make one word it was incorrect to call it an anagram so we called it a conundrum, meaning puzzle. If the truth be known the real reason was that *Countdown* Conundrum, with both words containing nine letters, fitted the studio set more tidily!

Under the circumstances Richard Whiteley and Ted Moult had done meritoriously during the regional shows. No personnel changes there!

We did decide that Ted needed help in Dictionary Corner: someone who knew how to read a dictionary, quickly and effectively, and pronounce judgement speedily, with conviction and total credibility, i.e. a lexicographer. Leeds University's English Department couldn't provide one. The department's representatives who sat with me during the regional shows did say that in their opinion *Chambers 20th Century Dictionary*, which we first used, was not the best dictionary for *Countdown*, as it contained too many obsolete and archaic words. They suggested we contact Oxford University Press. (My co-writer, Peter Newby, deals with this subject at some length in the next chapter.) One trip to Oxford and everything was settled. We would use the *Concise Oxford Dictionary* – the two volumed *Shorter* would, we thought, prove too cumbersome and time-consuming during a show when literally every second counts. That august body would also provide a team of lexicographers, much to the relief of Ted Moult who could then concentrate on coming up with longer words if possible and 'fill in' whilst his assistant was checking the validity of any words.

Now to the numbers game. We needed a statistician who could actually give a correct solution if the contestants failed. How I found Carol Vorderman is explained in a later chapter, but during the first networked series we alternated between Carol and Dr Linda Barret – yes, we had two statisticians. We also had two hostesses, the delectable Kathy Hytner, looking after the letters, and former Miss United Kingdom, Beverley Isherwood, displaying the numbers. Kathy took over both roles after one series.

The numerator in *Countdown* is called Cecil, an acronym for '*Countdown*'s electronic calculator in Leeds'. It was named after the aforementioned Cecil Korer, at that time our Commissioning Editor at Channel 4.

So the scene was set for recording the shows which had to be ready for October 1982. The first day was a disaster: for various reasons we didn't get one programme 'in the can'. Eventually we made the schedule, although every programme had to be edited as the opening titles were not ready when we recorded in studio – every show also overran our allotted running time. It's practically impossible to bring *Countdown* in on time, even now, as there are so many imponderables. How many words will the lexicographer have to check? Will the contestants get the same answer in the numbers games but with different methods, thus making Carol provide two workings-out? Will she then have to give them the correct solution? Will they get the Conundrum? Will Gyles Brandreth ever stop talking?

On 2 November, at 4.45 in the afternoon, *Countdown* became the first show to be transmitted on Channel 4 – a marvellous moment for Richard Whiteley. A stalwart of Yorkshire Television's regional programmes for 21 years, Richard had a previous rather dubious claim to fame throughout Britain, and indeed the world – the clip of video showing him being bitten by a ferret! Now he can be forever known as the first face on Channel 4.

But would that end up being a similarly dubious distinction? I've no idea what the immediate response was to *Countdown* or Channel 4 that day. A few days earlier I had fled to Tenerife for a break and it was there, on 4 November, that I read the reviews – Channel 4 was slated and so was *Countdown*.

On my return to Leeds, Frank Smith was far from depressed. Although Channel 4 was registering disappointing audience ratings, *Countdown* was featuring very strongly. Bit by bit, week by week, the audiences grew. Another series was commissioned, then another, but I was still disappointed with the ratings. By this time we'd been switched to 4.30 p.m. and I'd welcomed other celebrities to Dictionary Corner.

Frank Smith had left YTV by then and I was now working for the Director of Programmes, John Fairley. He seemed quite happy with *Countdown*'s progress, but I said that I wanted to make some serious changes in the next series. He told me to go ahead. We were due in studio in a month's time, but first Richard and I were invited to Monte Carlo as guests of Armand Jammot for the final of *Des Chiffres Et Des Lettres*. I decided I would tell Richard about my proposed changes there. What better way of discussing the future than over a pre-prandial Countdowner cocktail (Campari, grenadine and fresh orange with crushed ice), invented by Marcel Stellman, at the Hotel de Paris?

It was whilst we were there that YTV's Managing Director, Paul Fox, telephoned Richard with the marvellous news that *Countdown* had broken into Channel 4's list of top ten most successful shows. I decided the changes could wait.

Success breeds success. *Countdown* continued to feature regularly in Channel 4's top ten; indeed on numerous occasions all five daily shows have dominated the list. The rest, as they say, is history.

Amidst great celebrations the 500th show came and went. At the time of writing we are about to record the 1,000th show, a feat which will gain us entry into the *Guinness Book of Records* as the most prolific game show in the history of television.

In 1989 Channel 4 began broadcasting its daily morning section and once again *Countdown* was honoured to be in at the beginning, providing a five-minute mini version five days a week.

What of the future? How long can it last? All I can say is that *Des Chiffres Et Des Lettres* has been running in France now for 20 years; it's a way of life. Yorkshire Television is certainly committed to transmitting *Countdown* until the end of 1992. That would make ten years in all. After that who knows?

In the meantime *Countdown* continues and this book is a celebration of its success.

John Meade

Pignuts – and Why Not?

Countdown's word rules are eminently sensible. In essence, any English word capable of being written in the lower case and which can be confirmed in a specified dictionary is perfectly acceptable.[1]

Now consider the humble **pignut** (a nut found on North American hickory trees and often used to describe a variety of other nuts). A quite ordinary little word found in most dictionaries and valid for all word games, including Scrabble®, played in America, Canada, Australia, the West Indies, Indonesia, Israel and goodness knows where else – apart from the United Kingdom! For the U.K. Scrabble championship a particular dictionary has been selected and its treatment of **pignut** is curious to say the least.

On page 1101 of the 1988 edition of *Chambers English Dictionary* the word is uniquely hyphenated as 'pig-nut'. This hyphen invalidates the word for U.K. Scrabble and would also for *Countdown* – but only if you refer to page 1101 of Chambers! However, if you glance at page 56 in that same work you will find that **St. Anthony's nut** is another name for the unhyphenated **pignut**. This is not an isolated curiosity as you will also discover that *Chambers* has dozens of such ambiguities of a confusing nature. The *Concise Oxford Dictionary* used for the television version of *Countdown* is, thankfully, free of such problem areas though one has to admit that its word power is inferior to that of its 'big sister' the *Shorter Oxford* and its proud parent, the magnificent *Oxford English Dictionary*.

---

[1] The rules for television's *Countdown* specifically exclude those words in the *Concise Oxford* which are hyphenated, italicized (foreign words) or which incorporate an apostrophe. Equally invalid are abbreviations, prefixes, suffixes and combining forms.

The point is that one's choice of a dictionary will sometimes influence the validity or otherwise of words used in play. For this reason all discussion on words used in *Countdown* will be based on the *Concise Oxford* though, for added interest, other words will sometimes be mentioned. To illustrate this fact, consider the supreme anagram, the words capable of being produced from the following letters:

A	E	G	I	N	R	S	T

GROUP ONE   Those words valid for *Countdown* on the basis of being found in or implied by (e.g. adding an S to create a plural for a noun) the *Concise Oxford*:

ANGRIEST, GANISTER, GANTRIES, INGRATES, RANGIEST

GROUP TWO   Those words which are extant but not valid for the television version as they are not found in the *Concise Oxford*. They are, however, valid for the boxed version of the game but only if they appear in your particular dictionary. These include dialect and other marginal words:

ANGRITES, ASTRINGE, GAINTERS, GAIRTENS, GAITNERS, GASTERIN, GASTRINE, GRANITES[2], IGERANTS, NEGARITS, NEGRITAS, REASTING (also GAIRNEST, NARGIEST, RAINGEST, STRAEING, STREAING, TEARINGS which are suspect formations either discussed below or in the Glossary).

GROUP THREE   Whilst obsolete words are valid for the boxed version of *Countdown*, providing they appear as headwords in the dictionary you agree to accept, they are a special case as inferred forms of obsolete words need to be subjected to expert opinion. No standard popular dictionary provides sufficient evidence for this question to be considered and, therefore, they are treated in isolation. Group Three also includes proper nouns which are normally invalid for word games but are useful for crosswords:

---

[2]The *Concise* in common with many dictionaries defines only one type of **granite**, hence a plural under these circumstances is difficult to sustain. However, a granite is also the name for the stone used in the game of curling. Its plural is perfectly legitimate. Depending upon which dictionary you use, **granites** is either valid or invalid.

ARESTING,   GENITRAS,   GINESTAR,   GRANTISE,   GRETIANS,
INGESTAR,   INGREATS,   RATEINGS,   RATINGES,   REGISTAN,
RENIGATS,   RESTINGA,   SERGIANT,   STEARING,   STRAIGNE,
STRAINGE,   STRANGIE,   TANGIERS,   TARIENGS,   TIGRANES,
TIGREANS (the suspect formations include discussions on
ATERINGS, ERIGANTS, INRAGEST and STARINGE)

The Glossary at the back of the book will define the words of
Groups Two and Three not given in context. The question to
consider is why select the *Concise Oxford* when it is obviously
deficient in the perfectly acceptable Group Two words?

First of all it must be stressed that no one dictionary contains all
of these AEGINRST words, nor indeed the other possible anagrams
which take the potential to upwards, believe it or not, of 150 which
have been claimed for this combination of letters.

One hundred and fifty?

The amazing potential of the combination was first brought to
the attention of the American public as long ago as November 1925
when Howard B. McPherrin published his discovery of 21 perfect
AEGINRST anagrams in *The Enigma* magazine. In 1965, in his book
Language on Vacation, Dmitri Borgmann presented a collection of
65 'anagrams' but many of these were either words he had coined or
words he inferred from entries in various dictionaries. Borgmann,
unfortunately, went beyond the bounds of tolerance by ignoring the
conventions of grammatical history in a manner which *Countdown*'s
editorial experts would never countenance.

Whilst it is reasonable to infer current grammatical rules for
obsolete modern English (that which, in effect, expired after AD 1500),
one cannot justify the use of such endings as -ING, -IER, -IEST or
even a simple S as a plural to Middle English or, more especially,
even earlier forms of the language. Borgmann stretched his study
to the limits and, therefore, many of these 'words' have to be
discounted in a realistic compilation. Before 1500 one was more
likely to have, for example, N rather than S as the suffix for the
plural – OXEN is a relic of this practice – and, unless inflected forms
of this earlier language are specifically quoted, one cannot presume
a validity for anything other than the stated basic word.

Good dictionaries which include historical words make a clear
distinction between the words of this literary watershed. None

better than the *Oxford English Dictionary* (OED) which supplies specific dates. *Pears Advanced Word-Puzzler's Dictionary* differentiates by using the labels *obs* for obsolete modern and *Obs* for the words which expired before that significant, if arbitrary, year. *Funk & Wagnalls Standard Dictionary* prefers to describe the language of 1500–1700 as 'archaic' with that of previous times as 'obsolete'. By contrast, *Chambers English Dictionary* has no such distinction, apart from identifying many of its literary remnants with specific authors such as Spenser, Shakespeare and Milton. Any of its words labelled *obs* (obsolete) could, therefore, fall either side of 1500 and be subject to restrictive use as far as games players (or even anagram compilers!) are concerned. For the television programme, words found in the etymologies of the *Concise* are deemed invalid and this is the only place where its obsolete words occur. But, as these are noted without function, so they form no aspect of this study.

Now consider the Middle English word GRANTISE. Listed in Group Three it is found in both *Funk & Wagnalls* and the OED. Would, in 1330 (which is the last known date of literary usage), the plural have been 'GRANTISES' or 'GRANTISEN' or, indeed, some other form? To use the singular in games which permit obsolete words is sensible but to make inferences is highly questionable. To quote Borgmann's justification for two of his inclusions is to marvel at the man's erudition but, from a practical standpoint, one must reject his conclusions due to lack of recorded evidence:

'STARINGE – a Middle English form of STARING. The verb STARE came into Middle English from Old English. One of the Middle English spellings of the suffix -ING was -INGE. Since both the verb and the -INGE suffix form were used during the same period of time, it is an inescapable inference that STARINGE was a word sometimes used in Middle English.'

'INRAGEST – the second person singular present active indicative form of the verb INRAGE, an 18th century variation of the verb ENRAGE, customarily used after the pronoun "thou". At the time, the -EST inflected form was standard English.'

An 'inescapable inference' is not the same as a valid citation and one would also require a similar quote to prove the existence of a 'customarily used' archaic verbal inflection for a defunct spelling form.

To apply modern rules of grammar to words of modern English times – even if such words are obsolete – is reasonable and the games player may use these resultant forms without fear of contradiction. But, is the same true of archaic grammar applied to extant words? Consider two of Borgmann's further uses of the -EST inflection applied to exotic verbs found only in the superb *English Dialect Dictionary*:

GAIRNEST. This is justified by Borgmann as being a 'poetic' inflection of a Northumberland variation of the verb GIRN which was once standard English but is now retained only in Literary Scottish (an independent English language) and various northern English and Scottish dialects.
RAINGEST. A similar 'poetic' inflection of the Banff Scottish dialect verb RAING.

In the case of RAING this is a nonsense, as the *English Dialect Dictionary* specifically spells the potential RAINGEST as RAINGST in its solitary citation. As for GAIRN it is merely shown as the localized spelling in its definitive treatment of GIRN which has many citations (or quotes) and none can be found to justify his 'poetic licence'.

In theory both are still possible. So, how should the games player treat words of this ilk?

When the late Kenneth Williams dominated *Countdown*'s dictionary corner (in a manner that no subsequent celebrity guest has dared to emulate), he would declare with his inimitable scholastic vehemence, 'Archaic words are invalid.' An ambiguous statement, but true in two respects. Poetic inflections *unless specifically given in the dictionary* are inadmissable. Competitors who submit words which expired by 1700 (the technical sense used by *Funk & Wagnalls*) should be aware of the fact that words of this type do not appear in the *Concise*. Archaic words, as one normally understands the term, are perfectly acceptable.

For *Countdown*, or any other word game, the question would normally arise only with an archaic verbal inflection of an extant, standard English word. MAKETH, for example. This occurs in the well-known proverb: 'Manners maketh man'. The proverb's history is noted in the *Concise Oxford Dictionary of Proverbs* and its ultimate citation, dated 1966, actually uses the 'old-fashioned' spelling of MAKYTH. MAKETH is not specifically given in the *Concise* and we know how short the shrift Mr. Williams would give it – so, too, would any of the Oxford University Press editors who grace the dictionary corner. But, what about other experts in word game play?

It is invalid for Scrabble on either side of the Atlantic. They use reference works, discussed elsewhere, which have a policy of noting all acceptable verbal inflections and, for the verb MAKE, the only permitted forms are MAKE, MADE, MAKES and MAKING. The Pears Word Games Society, which uses any available dictionary, would permit the word *but only if it can be shown to exist within the covers of an acceptable reference work*. This society plays many different word games, some of which will be discussed in due course, but its attitude towards the acceptability or otherwise of any specific word, mirrors that of the adjudicators for *Countdown* or Scrabble. Consequently, it would reject STARINGE, INRAGEST, GAIRNEST, RAINGEST and, apart from its games based on proverbs, MAKETH.

Two other groups of words which form part of Borgmann's AEGINRST compilation are worthy of examination in greater detail. The first of these is a pair with a supposed identical meaning, STRAEING and STREAING.

For this pair his authority is the second edition of *Webster's New International Dictionary* (Unabridged, 1953). This gives both STRAE and STREA as dialect forms of the word STRAW. It provides no clue as to the function of the words thus they *could* be forms of STRAW in its function as a verb. *Webster's 2nd* has the verb STRAW with a sense of 'to strew' or cover with something 'strewn'. It notes the verb as being 'archaic or dialect'. On this evidence a player might argue that both STRAEING and STREAING are reasonable assumptions. However, this is not always true and it certainly is not in the case of these two words.

The *English Dialect Dictionary* reveals the following:

STRAE is a South Lanarkshire Scottish dialect spelling of STRAW. STREA is a Northumberland, Cumberland and York-shire spelling of STRAW.

STRAW as a verb in the given sense is not known in South Lanarkshire or Cumberland, whilst in Northumberland and Yorkshire the use of STREA for the verb is not applicable. Technically, this verb applies to a different root of the language which now finds common spelling as the word STRAW. A verb does exist for which

STRAE and STREA might, technically, qualify but this exists only in Lincolnshire and has nothing to do with strewing but with straw itself.

STRAEING and STREAING are both invalid, not only for word games but for a definitive study of the AEGINRST potential.

The literate games player should beware of making similar assumptions as dictionaries do not separate headwords for appearance's sake but for sound etymological reasons. Consider the word TEAR.

The *Concise* separates this into two different entries. The first defines the action as 'pulling apart with some force' and refers its adjective, TEARING, to this entry. Incidentally, it gives an archaic verbal inflection TARE (where the modern form is TORE) within this main entry. Its second entry is concerned with the clear, saline liquid which serves to moisten the eye and it is in this sense that you will discover TEARINGS defined in the Glossary. The two senses of STRAW discussed above are equally distinct, despite having a similarity of pronunciation.

Now, another set of words. ATERINGS, RATEINGS and RATINGES:

ATERINGS. Borgmann cites *Webster's New International Dictionary* (first edition, unabridged, 1919) as his authority, with the OED as providing supplementary evidence. Here I am at a disadvantage as I do not have access to this particular edition of that great American dictionary but the fact that he considered it necessary to support his argument by reference to the OED is significant. Borgmann states that ATERING is a 'gerund of the verb ATER, an obsolete variation of the verb ATTER, to poison, embitter (and) the OED identifies ATTER as a 13th century verb'.

The OED has no such gerund and it gives a history of the verb from circa AD 885 (when it was used by King Alfred the Great) to circa 1400. Thus it is reasonable to suppose that it expired in Middle English times and, therefore, a games player cannot justify this supposed plural. The 1919 edition could prove me wrong, but I doubt it.

RATEINGS. The plural of RATING in a spelling form exclusive to Pepys in 1667. The sense is specifically that of the action of administering a rebuke, though the OED (the quoted authority) carries no citations which exhibit a plural. Is a plural logical?

RATINGES. The plural of RATINGE, an earlier form of RATING and used in an Act of Parliament dated 1534. The sense being the levying of a rate and, technically, the same word which takes a natural plural in the nautical term NAVAL RATINGS (sailors), though that expression was coined centuries later. Once again, can one justify the addition of an S?

In both of these cases the games player is on the safe side of 1500 and a plural is a fair assumption. Therefore, RATEINGS and RATINGES may be deemed valid.

Sadly, Borgmann died in 1985 though this erratic genius had continued to research the supreme anagram. Among his more reasonable discoveries not given above are:

ARGENTIS   The first word of the term ARGENTIS QUINASEPTOL, an antiseptic mentioned in a technical publication on chemical synonyms and trade names. Its synonym being ARGENTOL.

GINESTRA   An Italian name for the broom, a yellow-flowered shrub, given in volume 1 of OED *Supplement* (1972). Treated as foreign, it has the potential for assimilation into the English language.

GERSAINT   The surname of a French antiquary who died in 1750 and deemed worthy of recording in *A Dictionary of Universal Biography*.

INERT GAS   One of a group of noble gases which include helium, neon and argon.

SARGENTI   A foodstuff trademark given registration number 640,117 and found in *The Trademark Register of the United States* (1974).

SEAT RING   A replaceable ring that forms the seat of a valve.

ST. REGINA   A virgin and martyr whose feast day falls on 7 September.

TARGESIN   The trademark name of an antiseptic.

But, contrast those with these typical examples of 'words' which he considered capable of being inferred from the dictionary:—

ASTERING   from ASTERE, a pre-1500 form of ASTIR.

GNAISTER   One who gnaists. GNAIST being a pre-1500 form of GNAST. (See Glossary.)

GRAINEST   Another of the archaic verbal inflections. This one for the verb GRAIN, to turn into grains.

GRIATNES   A combination of GRIAT (a Kentish Middle English form of GREAT) together with -NES (a Middle English form of -NESS) to produce GREATNESS.

REGAINST   Yet another archaic verbal inflection.

SIGNATER   More signate. A presumed comparative to suggest that something is more designated or more identified!

If, as most of us have, you have had arguments over the Scrabble board, imagine what it must have been like for Mrs. Dmitri A. Borgmann of Dayton, Washington, USA, if she ever played a quiet game with a husband such as hers!

His research even extended to telephone directories where his more bizarre offerings comprised combinations of initials and surnames as well as plurals of surnames. But he ultimately descended to the realms of pure farce with such AEGINRST inclusions as TEN RIGAS which he maintained, quite seriously, was 'ten cities all named Riga' – providing that his readers could find nine more to supplement the one he had already discovered in his atlas!

By 1976 thanks to additional research by Borgmann, Dwight Ripley and series six *Countdown* champion Darryl Francis, the total (which incorporates all bar one of the examples given above) had reached 131. In 1977, Sir Jeremy Morse added a further 21 Latin examples to the list which already had other foreign language words culled from the etymological aspects of English language dictionaries – most notably the *Oxford English Dictionary*. And, finally, in 1979 the New Zealand wordsmith, Jeff Grant, added a further seven constructions which complied with Borgmann's criteria together with one genuine dictionary word, GENITRAS.

Obviously the foreign words can be dismissed from serious consideration in any word game played in English and the whole of the McPherrin/Borgmann/Ripley/Francis/Morse/Grant research can be boiled down to around 30 words as far as serious players of most word games are concerned. Equally significantly, those words are still subject to dispute as to which are acceptable or otherwise for *any* word game, let alone *Countdown*.

But, if one assumes that these anagrams distilled from more than a hundred reference works were all available in one bookcase in *Countdown*'s dictionary corner, imagine how long it would take to prove the existence or otherwise of just one word.

One has to be practical and the most sensible practical decision is to limit validity to those words contained in a single dictionary.

But, why the *Concise*?

Quite simply because it is good and has none of the potential absurdities which can arise from consideration of the obsolete and, of course, because it knows how to spell **pignuts**.

Peter Newby

Aardvarks

(A LITTLE AARDVARK NEVER HURT ANYONE)

The AARDVARK began life in the *Oxford English Dictionary* as AARD-VARK though the hyphen has subsequently been removed by all other works in the *Oxford* family.

Hyphens are going out of fashion – their heyday was the eighteenth and nineteenth centuries when many previously unhyphenated words developed this style – and the new edition of the *Concise Oxford* (due for publication within a matter of weeks of the appearance of this book) will reflect these changes quite considerably. Many *Countdown* fans, however, will retain their existing editions whilst other readers will possess other dictionaries such as the *Collins Concise* or, if they are Scrabble players, *Chambers English*.

As Countdowners may be puzzled by some of the rulings given in the dictionary corner – hyphens invalidate words for the game – so this whole question will be considered in detail. To do this it is necessary to compare and contrast these three dictionaries giving both their strengths and their weaknesses.

Collins Concise (1984). An excellent dictionary, clearly presented. As error-free as any work of this magnitude can be. Completely up-to-date in its treatment of words capable of being hyphenated. Inferior in word power from the standpoint of word game players.

Concise Oxford (7th edition, 1982). An excellent dictionary with a fairly clear presentation. As error-free as any work of this magnitude can be. Reasonably up-to-date concerning words capable of being hyphenated. Fair in word power from the game player's standpoint.

Chambers English (1988). A mishmash of superior word power with errors of fact and scholarship on hundreds of its pages. Its

30

treatment of hyphenated words borders on the ludicrous. PIGNUTS is only one example of this curious attitude, others are words such as APPLEJACK and SANDHOG. These are words of American origin, unhyphenated in American dictionaries, yet *Chambers* just has to be different. Even with the assistance of its Scrabble-playing reader-ship, who have pointed out some of the more mind-boggling curiosities of its immediate predecessor (*Chambers 20th Century Dictionary*), it is still a minefield to be negotiated at one's own peril. Scrabble players managed to have the word YIBBLES transferred to the correct alphabetical position in the book. In an earlier edition of the *Chambers* 20C it was found buried away within the entry for the word – wait for it – ABLE! At least they managed to have a cross-reference inserted in the later edition.

But *Chambers English* has a new YIBBLES. This is the word AFLAJ. AFLAJ only appears under F where it is given as the plural of FALAJ. It is suggestive of a typographical error despite being repeated in the book *Official Scrabble Words*, a publication based on *Chambers* and deemed necessary because of the ambiguities of its parent work. Not that this is any more reliable as it has, for example, the plural of MUREX as MUREXS, though giving the two correct plurals of MUREXES and MURICES. Scrabble players have to be equally illiterate when providing a plural for STRATUS. As *Chambers* does not provide one so the *Official Scrabble Words* comes to the rescue with STRATUSES, whereas other dictionaries – the *Concise Oxford*, *Collins Concise*, *The Official Scrabble Players Dictionary* (for American players), *Funk & Wagnalls Standard* etc. – all give one absolute plural, STRATI! However, AFLAJ is not an impossible plural as the *Concise* has one just as remarkable, AREG. The singular, believe it or not, is ERG. The difference between accepting AREG and questioning AFLAJ lies in the fact that not only does the *Concise* carry a cross-reference from A (AREG) to E (ERG) but one can have faith in the *Oxford* scholarship. By contrast, *Chambers* carries no such cross-reference from A (AFLAJ) to F (FALAJ) and had I not had confirmation of AFLAJ's existence from a 1976 newspaper article – no other dictionary carries AFLAJ/FALAJ – so I might have supposed it to be another *Chambers* error. (*Chambers* entry for TARPON, for example, has this member of the eel family 'akin' to the totally unrelated herring. Other examples will be given in due course but suffice it that *Pears Advanced Word-Puzzlers Dictionary* considered it necessary to devote four whole pages

(184–187) to the examination of the different *types* of error found in *Chambers*!)

To see the hyphens in context the letter B has been selected to contrast the treatment by *Collins Concise*, the 1982 *Concise Oxford* and *Chambers*. Only words of up to nine letters have been considered – simply because the larger words are irrelevant to *Countdown* – but above this level the contrast is even more pronounced. An asterisk indicates that this particular word does not occur in the specified dictionary.

Those compounds hyphenated in the *Concise Oxford* column and appearing in italics will become non-hyphenated single words in the new 1990 edition. Thus, they will now be valid for *Countdown*. For example, BARGE-POLE.

Those compounds with a bracketed hyphen will now be shown as two words. Thus, BIRD(-)TABLE will remain invalid for *Countdown*. Unfortunately, others will remain hyphenated despite the fact that a work as respected as *Collins Concise* rejects such pedantic and, in most cases, totally unnecessary forms. In the main, *Collins* and *Oxford* tend to be consistent even if they are at variance with each other but *Chambers* is in a league of its own. *Collins* has **bell pull** and **bell push**, *Oxford* has **bell-pull** and **bell-push**. By contrast, *Chambers* has **bell-pull** and **bellpush**! Anyway, see what else you can find and if you can make sense of this typical compilation you understand the language far better than me.

Collins Concise	*Concise Oxford*	*Chambers*
backboard	backboard	back-board
backcloth	backcloth	back-cloth
backcomb	backcomb	back-comb
backdate	backdate	back-date
baldhead	baldhead	bald-head
ball boy	ballboy	*
bandbox	bandbox	band-box
band saw	band-saw	band-saw
bangtail	bangtail	bang-tail
bankbook	bank-book	bank-book
bank note	banknote	bank-note
barbell	barbell	bar-bell
bargepole	*barge-pole*	bargepole

Collins Concise	Concise Oxford	Chambers
[1]barnstorm	barnstorm	barnstorm
baseline	baseline	base-line
bathtub	bath-tub	bathtub
battle-axe	battleaxe	battle-axe
beachhead	*beach-head*	beachhead
bear hug	bear-hug	*
bedjacket	bedjacket	bed-jacket
bedroll	bedroll	bed-roll
*	bedtable	bed-table
*	beechwood	beech-wood
*	beerhouse	beer-house
bellbird	*bell-bird*	bell-bird
bellboy	bellboy	bell-boy
bell buoy	bell-buoy	bell-buoy
bell pull	bell-pull	bell-pull
bell push	bell-push	bellpush
bell tent	bell-tent	bell-tent
bellyache	bellyache	belly-ache
bellyband	*belly-band*	belly-band
bench mark	*bench-mark*	bench-mark
birdbath	bird-bath	birdbath
bird call	bird-call	birdcall
bird strike	bird-strike	bird strike
bird table	bird(-)table	bird-table
birth rate	birthrate	birth-rate
blackfly	blackfly	black fly
black spot	blackspot	black spot
blood bath	blood(-)bath	blood-bath
blood heat	blood-heat	bloodheat
bloodworm	bloodworm	blood-worm
blowfish	*blow-fish*	*
bluebird	*blue-bird*	bluebird
blue chip	blue-chip	blue-chip
boathook	boat-hook	boat-hook
boathouse	boat-house	boathouse
boatload	boatload	boat-load
boat train	boat-train	boat-train
bobsleigh	bob-sleigh	bobsleigh

Collins Concise	Concise Oxford	Chambers
body blow	body-blow	body blow
[2]body-line	bodyline	bodyline/body-line
bogbean	bog-bean	bogbean
boldface	bold-face	*
bolt hole	bolt-hole	bolthole
bombsight	bomb-sight	*
bookplate	book-plate	bookplate
bootjack	*boot-jack*	bootjack
box kite	box(-)kite	box-kite
brain wave	brainwave	brain-wave
brake shoe	brake(-)shoe	brake-shoe
brake van	brake(-)van	brake-van
breadfruit	*bread-fruit*	breadfruit
break up	breakup	break up
brick red	brick-red	brick-red
briefcase	*brief-case*	brief-case
buckhorn	buck-horn	buckhorn
bun fight	bun(-)fight	bun-fight
bushbaby	bush-baby	bush-baby
bushbuck	*bush-buck*	bush-buck
butternut	butter-nut	butternut
*	byname	by-name

---

[1]Whilst all three agree upon BARNSTORM *Chambers* has BARN-STORMER!
Both *Collins* and *Oxford* have BARNSTORMER. This is not unique as *Chambers*
also has such as NINE-PIN and NINEPINS!

[2]The word **bodyline** was specifically coined as one word to save money on the
cost of a telegram by an English newspaper reporter during the infamous
bodyline tour of Australia by the M.C.C. To hyphenate this word is to destroy
its historically significant origin.

The question arises as to why the 1990 *Concise Oxford* will have
modernized some words but not others. Why, for example, now
have **bushbuck** but still retain **bush-baby**? The answer is usage by
those whose opinions one can respect. Lexicographers refer to
these usages as citations and *The Encyclopedia of the Animal World*
might well have been one such authority in this respect as it refers
to these creatures in just this manner.

Essentially, however, it is largely a matter of personal preference and, whilst I prefer **bushbaby** and will write it in this form secure in the knowledge that the editors of *Collins Concise* will support me, I cannot bring myself to agree with the American scholarship of *The Official Scrabble Players Dictionary*. In this particular work they have words which look strange to the British eye without a natural hyphen. Would you have known what these words were if you had not already been forewarned:–

REEMBARK, REEMIT, REENTER, REERECT?

Hyphens are still necessary in some respects – I would hate to be perceived as John Meade's COW RITER if **co-writer** ever followed COWORKER into that American work as a single, unhyphenated word. The *English Dialect Dictionary* contains some delightful words which would look ludicrous if ever they were similarly 'Americanized'. Consider the names of these two flowers. The first is a Kentish term for the cuckoo-pint or wild arum whilst the second is a Lincolnshire expression for the pansy:–

KITTY-COME-DOWN-THE-LANE-JUMP-UP-AND-KISS-ME
MEET-HER-IN-THE-ENTRY-KISS-HER-IN-THE-BUTTERY

and both deserve a wider audience. Garden centre owners, please note.

The second question which arises is that of 'missing' words.

Collins Concise can be excused. It has sacrificed word power for clarity and avoids wherever possible, the confusing system of having some supplementary words under a single heading whilst others have their own individual entry. For example, words and terms related to BLOOD.

Very sensibly the only 'blood relatives' it has within the main entry for BLOOD are those expressions suffixed with this word – BAD BLOOD, COLD BLOOD etc. All words and terms prefixed blood – BLOOD BROTHER, BLOODSHED etc. – are given space-consuming individual entries and, in consequence, something has had to give. Therefore, it cannot be censured for not having such as BEDTABLE or BEERHOUSE. The other two works, however, lump their 'BLOOD words' together in huge, often confusing, single entries, though the 1982 *Concise Oxford* is less compact than *Chambers* in this particular respect. The 1990 edition will unscramble still further but whether this is an improvement or not remains to be seen. One can only hope that it will be as logical as *Collins* without too much sacrifice of word power.

Chambers, apart from its silly hyphens, can have no excuse for 'missing' words as it has a deliberate policy of giving as many headwords as possible. In consequence it has such wordsmith ammunition as CLOACINAL, GANDERISM, ISMATIC, LACERANT and SCOTIAN, all of which are deemed extant standard English. Unless the editors of *Chambers* have citations unknown to other lexicographers these are not only nonce words but, in the case of SCOTIAN, an obsolete nonce word! (See Glossary for a definition of a nonce word.) How *Chambers* can justify these at the expense of everyday words such as BRASSWARE, BRAINPOWER or BRAINWORK is beyond me. It abounds with all manner of disguised non-standard terms and to illustrate this point, consider its treatment of CHAUNTRESS.

Chambers has this as an undefined noun within its main entry for CHANT. The inference being that the word is extant and common sense should supply the meaning. Do you know what it means? It baffled me – until I consulted the *Oxford English Dictionary*.

CHAUNTRESS happens to be Milton's unique way of spelling CHANTRESS, a rare word for a female singer. He used it in his poem *Il Penseroso*, written in 1632 and no one else has bothered to use it since! By contrast, *Chambers* has the word DISPLODE 'exclusive' to John Milton, but Swift (1667–1745) also used it and so have other writers much nearer to our own times.

If any reader considers that I have taken a few extreme examples then he or she can prove these to be *typical* by the simple expedient of opening up *Chambers* at any page and finding words which it assigns 'exclusively' to Spenser, Shakespeare or Milton. Now see what the *Oxford English Dictionary* says about the same words. You will even find Spenser or Shakespeare 'exclusives' that *neither ever used* but, what is even more ridiculous, some of these were first recorded in the literature of Anglo-Saxon times and they are still extant!

John Meade, the producer of *Countdown* and co-writer of this book, and his team frequently come across people who say that a dis-allowed word appears in *Chambers*. They are also aware of the accuracy of scholarship which makes the *Concise Oxford* such an admirable work of reference.

Countdown is for people with BRAINPOWER even if they cannot utilize it – nine letters is the game's limit – but at least their dictionary has been compiled with BRAINWORK!

Apart from modernizing many of its hyphenated words, what other changes are likely to occur in the new *Concise* which will influence the validity decisions of the programme?

The word GLASNOST will make its debut in the 8th edition as will a number of the uglier coinings of the last few years. Some words will have to disappear in order to accommodate new ones and, sadly, the most likely candidates are the delightful archaic words.

MANWARD is an archaic adjective which is of interest to games players as it is valid for both *Countdown* and Scrabble in America but not available for the U.K. Scrabble championship. YCLEPT is the last remaining word prefixed Y- and it would be a tragedy if this followed NEW YORK's anagram, YWROKEN, into the comparative oblivion of either the larger or specialist dictionaries. Once the language abounded with these curious words but only YBLENT, YCLAD, YCLEPT, YWROKEN and YWROUGHT are extant, with YCLEPT still gracing the pages of *Chambers*, the *Concise* and *Collins Concise*, so still available to the public at large. The Y- is a now meaningless prefix and the sense of the word is obtained by ignoring it. Thus YCLAD is CLAD and YWROUGHT is WROUGHT but, for convenience, the others will be defined in the Glossary.

Fortunately, MANWARD and YCLEPT will be retained but, sadly, a different word of great interest to games players will disappear. This is QUIXOTIZE. Unavailable in either of the official reference works used for Scrabble championships throughout the English-speaking world it has the capacity for establishing the world record for the highest single score likely to be made in a single move. The current record is 392 points achieved by utilizing an existing letter on the board and thereby creating an 8-letter word with the seven tiles that the player had available.

For QUIXOTIZE to be played, two of its letters must already be present on the board. For example, TI is a genuine 2-letter word and this could be turned into the record-breaking 9-letter word by the addition of a player's letters either side of it.

The ideal position for this is the first nine squares of an outermost line in order to maximize the points multiplication factor. Consider the top left-hand corner of the board and the placing of the Q on the triple-word square. The natural run will have the X (worth 8 points) on the double-letter value square so increasing its value to 16 points. The Z will now fall on the vital second triple-word square thus creating the marvellous multiplication factor of 'times nine'. This is how it would appear:

$$Q \; U \; I \; X \; O \; T \; I \; Z \; E$$
$$(10 \; 1 \; 1 \; 16 \; 1 \; 1 \; 1 \; 10 \; 1) \times 3 \times 3 + 50$$

With the 50 bonus points for using all of one's seven available letters this produces a grand total of 429 points for one spectacular and perfectly feasible move.

Another good Scrabble word (equally unavailable to championship players using either of their official references), and due for deletion from the *Concise Oxford*, is BOXCALF. So now, if you wish to score a minimum of 21 points:—

$$B \; O \; X \; C \; A \; L \; F$$
$$3 \; 1 \; 8 \; 3 \; 1 \; 1 \; 4$$

(you only get the 50 bonus points if you play all seven yourself) then you will have to use *Collins Concise* as it is not *that* deficient in word power.

Perhaps the Oxford University Press will revive such wordsmith words as these should it commence work on its 'missing' dictionary, the one which it needs to complete the range by having a word power greater than its *Concise* but not as scholarly as its *Shorter*. Certainly, an accurately produced work of this order is urgently required by literate players of word games in the U.K. and, as an inventor of many published word games, I for one would love to be able to recommend a single reference work for all of mine. The *Concise* suits many games but words are valuable ammunition and I mourn the consignment into limbo of QUIXOTIZE.

However, the *Countdown* changes for the better will include the removal of unnecessary hyphens, the accepted assimilation into English of some of the words currently deemed foreign and the advent of GLASNOST.

The AARD-VARK is dead. Long live the AARDVARK. *Countdown* enters the '90s with the '90s newest and best dictionary for everyday language.

Peter Newby

Target Practice

To become a champion of *Countdown*, it is essential to master the techniques of word play, and, by far, the most enjoyable way of achieving this is to become acquainted with other word games.

It is no secret that many of the best *Countdown* performers subsequently feature quite prominently in other television contests based upon words and, in most cases, they are expert word game players. Long before they attempt to produce the 8-letter or 9-letter top-scoring *Countdown* words they have developed a natural expertise with words in general.

Some are masters of Scrabble, others are crossword addicts. For example, the very first *Countdown* champion, Joyce Cansfield, is not only a former U.K. Scrabble champion but also compiles many of the crosswords for *The Times*. Not that one has to be as expert as this to succeed, but one does need to be aware of two factors – the 'shape' of words and the 'value' of individual letters. The playing of certain word games develops these skills quite naturally.

Members of the Pears Word Games Society (an international association of games players) regularly challenge each other with pencil and paper contests that are not only great fun but, in the long run, are excellent training material for anyone who wishes to be a Countdowner. The following are just four of the games they play, together with 'target scores'. If you equal or better these targets then you are well on the way to being a candidate for the programme.

1 SHELLING PEAS

This is a competition devised by the Hollywood film actor Maxwell Caulfield and is normally played as a challenge to a gathering of people all of whom are attempting to achieve the highest individual score. Two targets are given:

(a) group one words (those in the *Concise*)
(b) groups one and two words (any dictionary)

and your test is to make the group one target without penalization. The Society plays to groups one and two and even permits group three words (the obsolete) but here we are concerned with *Countdown* and, essentially, everyday words.

The object of the game is to add the letter P to a given word and so create a different word. Each different word containing a P scores a point on a basis of one point per P.

For example IT.

As PIT it scores 1 point, but as it can also be TIP so that scores a total of 2 points. PIPT is how PIPPED was once written. Is it so written today? If it is, then your score is now 4 points. But, if it is *not* then your score (assuming that you have PIT, TIP, PIPT) is not 2 points but nil points as the two you gained with PIT and TIP have been lost by the two incorrect Ps of PIPT. That is the gamble. How safe is your chosen word?

The following nine words were set as a test at a meeting of the Society which included two former television Countdowners and one who failed the audition. Their scores will be given in due course, but give yourself ten minutes and see what you can produce:

Score

IT	....
AT	....
TO	....
AY	....
ALE	....
TOE	....
DEAL	....
EDITOR	....
STEREO	....

Total _____

The group one target score will be that achieved by the lower scoring of the two Countdowners. Group one words and a full list of groups one and two words will be detailed at the end of this chapter. However, from a *Countdown* point of view, group two words must be *deducted* from your score should you have included any of these in your Shelling Peas submission. If you can make the target you are a potential *Countdown* contestant.

2 FRENCH CROSSWORDS

This is a delightful game and an exceedingly popular contest between two people. For practical purposes, only words found in the *Concise* are considered and the target score is computed accordingly.

Keeping their workings secret from each other, the players draw simple 5 × 5 grids. They take turns in calling out any letter of their choice and both placing it in any square of their choice. For example, suppose that player number one begins by having (say) the letter T. This could be put in squares as different as:

Player One   *Player Two*

In consequence, player number two may choose (say) the letter H, with the following results:

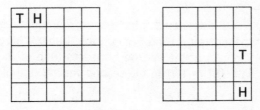

An R, given by player one, might be deployed in this manner:

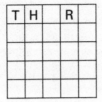 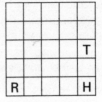

Eventually the squares are completed and there is no objection to a letter being repeated. The winner is the person with the higher score achieved in the following fashion:

(a) Each 5-letter word in either a horizontal or vertical plane scores 6 points. This is the bonus score.

(b) Assuming that no 5-letter word has been achieved on a line then the biggest single word on that line is scored with
4 points for a 4-letter word
3 points for a 3-letter word
2 points for a 2-letter word
but only one word per line may be scored.

Our completed squares with their consequent scores might look like this:

Note that it is immaterial which word you quote for scoring purposes, so long as it is valid. For example, either WAN or ANA will score the 3 points in the second horizontal line of the left-hand square as will HAT or TOT in the second vertical line of that same square.

All words must be lower case and found in the agreed dictionary in the event of a dispute. Abbreviations are not permitted, but there is no objection to slang or plurals. Players of *Countdown* standard, score consistently in excess of 45 points. A minimum of 46 points is your target.

Obviously, this same game can be played with grids of different sizes and the 9 × 9 version is described in the following chapter. But the basic 5 × 5 game is a great challenge and well worth playing with any friend who enjoys word games. Any version, including the 5 × 5, is known as **competitive word squares** though 'French Crosswords' is sometimes used as a distinguishing name for the smallest game in this series.

3 Q-DYE

Q-Dye is a solitaire game of delightful frustration which the taller of the two writers of this book devised especially for word game enthusiasts at the Japanese University of that name.

Q-Dye uses the concept of word ladders i.e. changing HEAD to TAIL one letter at a time and, each time, ensuring that a valid word is created:

```
H E A D
H E A L
T E A L
T E I L
T A I L
```

But it is not as simple as that. The test of Q-Dye is to begin with a duplicated 4-letter word and, from this, produce an anagram of an 8-letter word. For example, the challenge is to get to PARADISE by a double ladder of the word QUIZ:

```
Q U I Z        Q U I Z
Q U I T        Q U I N
S U I T        R U I N
S L U T        R A I N
```

This has the letter S of PARADISE in the first column and R, A and I of PARADISE in the second column. One move later and the combination of

```
S L A T        R E I N
```

now has the S and A in the first column and the R, E and I in the second column. So it will continue until one has such combinations as PEAR + SAID or RAID + APES at which point the goal has been achieved.

Q-Dye has one infuriating little rule, and that is that no word may be repeated in an individual column, so one could *not* have such a series of plays as:

S A I D
S A I L
S A I D
S A I L
S A I D etc.

whilst attempting to produce such as PEAR, PARE, REAP or RAPE in the twin column.

However, whilst Q–Dye in its pure form is a little gem of word play, it is not to be recommended as a *Countdown* training game. A simpler form of Q-Dye is ideal for this purpose.

Imagine that one begins with QUIZ + QUIZ and just continues making changes until *any* 8-letter word has emerged. Test yourself on this sample run and see if you achieve the target which a potential Countdowner would have to obtain. At which pair of 4-letter words does the first 8-letter word arrive? Is there a second combination or even a third? Only group one words qualify.

Q U I Z	Q U I Z
Q U I T	Q U I N
S U I T	R U I N
S L I T	R A I N
S L A T	R E I N
S E A T	V E I N
S E A L	V E I L
S E A R	T E I L
S E A S	T E A L
S E T S	R . E A L

Answers will be given at the end of this chapter but the important aspect of this exercise is to recognize which are and are not 'good' combinations. A top player, even if he or she does not discern an 8-letter word immediately, would still know which combinations have the potential and which do not.

Once you have mastered the technique at 8-letter word level then you may care to try the same exercise for 9-letter words but beware of the given initial pair. They produce two 9-letter words, but is either of these in group one?

START HERE

The given initial pairs (QUIZ + QUIZ for 8-letter words and START + HERE for 9-letter words) have been chosen not merely on a basis of reasonable aptness but, essentially, because they have the capacity for a variety of unlimited destinations. If you wish to begin with an original initial pair (say a 6-letter word + a 3-letter word) you may well discover that an abrupt ending to a particular column soon pertains. In selecting initial pairs test them for flexibility by considering both words separately. For example, COUNT + DOWN. DOWN presents no problems but COUNT will soon have you in difficulty. By contrast FAR + SHORES can, literally, take you any-where. Each letter of FAR can be changed immediately (WAR, FIR, FAT) as can SHORES (CHORES, STORES, SHARES, SHAVES, SHORTS, SHORED).

However, this pure *Countdown* aspect of Q-Dye will be discussed in greater detail in the chapter *Alternative* Countdown *Word Games*, beginning on page 50 in which it is shown as a two-person contest.

4 PENTERY WEB

This is a two-person game, normally played with anagrams of 6-letter words as these are relatively easy to produce. However, Countdowners would benefit most if the game is played at the 9-letter word level which is more fun but requires a knowledge of anagrams beyond the scope of anyone but the specialist.

Fortunately, a goodly selection of these – all valid for *Countdown* – concludes the chapter in this book on the subject of anagrams and so you and an opponent have the necessary ammunition at your disposal for a fascinating challenge in word skill.

Suppose that you turn to page 79 and select the pair RACIALIST/ SATIRICAL. Your opponent will now attempt to discover both of these words in a contest which resembles a version of Hangman. He or she is given the minimum reasonable information but you will attempt to be as crafty as possible in order to reduce the number of points which your opponent can score.

Having made your selection you now write down two sets of nine dots, Hangman-style, then add three *identical* letters to each set:

.A.I...I..   ..I..I.A.

The first set has one of the As and both Is of RACIALIST and the second set has the *same* choice of letters for SATIRICAL. Twelve dots remain unknown. If your opponent can guess both words at this stage he or she scores one point per uncovered dot. Twelve dots, 12 points.

This is most unlikely, so you now add another letter to both sets (the same letter in each case) and the points available are reduced to ten:

.ACI..I..   ..I..ICA.

Assuming continued failure, 8 points are available for:

.ACI..IS.   S..I..ICA.

Six points for:

.ACIA.IS.   SA.I..ICA.

Four points for:

.ACIAL.IS.   SA.I..ICAL

Two points for:

.ACIALIST   SATI..ICAL

and if your opponent is still baffled, play the game with someone else!

In the course of play a contestant may either 'pass' (most will do so at the earlier stages) or else guess at one or both words.

Immediately a player makes a wrong guess – be it at one or both words – you make no comment but simply add an additional letter to both words. Should a player correctly guess (say) RACIALIST but has not yet determined SATIRICAL you neither confirm nor deny the guess. You wait until the opponent makes either an error on the second word or is forced to pass. This is unlikely with the pair

RACIALIST/SATIRICAL but a combination such as APPEALING/ LAGNIAPPE is very likely to have the opponent in utter confusion.

You should agree the amount of time allowed for guessing and, ideally, your best opponent is one who plays at a similar pace to your own. Quick thinkers and plodders soon get on each other's nerves at any game and Pentery Web is no exception. Admittedly, points are at stake, but if you are training for the programme then speed rather than a leisurely approach is to be preferred.

The target is to score consistently high points.

Peter Newby

ANSWERS

Shelling Peas (page 40)

		points
IT	PIT, TIP	2
AT	APT, PAT, TAP	3
TO	OPT, POT, TOP	3
AY	PAY, YAP, YAPP, PAPPY	7
ALE	LEAP, PALE, PEAL, PLEA, APPLE	6
TOE	POET, TOPE, POPPET	5
DEAL	PALED, PEDAL, PLEAD, DAPPLE, LAPPED	7
EDITOR	DIOPTER, DIOPTRE, PERIDOT	3
STEREO		nil
		36

Of the 36 points available from group one words the lower scoring of the two former *Countdown* players achieved 25 points and this must be your target. However, this has to be 25 points *net* as you must deduct points for errors which include the following group two words that take the combined total to an amazing 64 points:

		additional points
IT		nil
AT		nil
TO		nil
AY	PYA	1
ALE	ALPE, LEPA, PELA, PAPLE, PAPPLE	8
TOE	PETO, POTE, EPOPT	4
DEAL	PADLE, APPLED, PALPED, PLAPPED	8
EDITOR	PROTEID, PTEROPID	3
STEREO	PEPPERPOTS (It is hyphenated in the *Concise* but not in all dictionaries – see Glossary)	4
		28

Q-Dye (page 43)

(a) 8-letter words
The available group one words are as follows:
SLAT + REIN   ENTRAILS, LATRINES, RATLINES, TRENAILS
SEAT + VEIN   NAIVETES
SEAR + TEIL   ATELIERS, EARLIEST, REALTIES
SETS + REAL   STEALERS, TEARLESS, TESSERAL

(b) 9-letter words
START + HERE   both RATHEREST (see Glossary) and SHATTERER are group two words and, as such, would be disallowed on the programme.

The targets are to have discovered at least one word in each of the SLAT + REIN, SEAR + TEIL, SETS + REAL pairings and have refused the opportunity for playing either START + HERE word.

Alternative Countdown Word Games

Two previously mentioned games are described. These are competitive word squares (French Crosswords) and Q-Dye taken to a more demanding level – that of the 9-letter word base. The expert's 9 × 9 version of competitive word squares has its own distinguishing name of Arepo, whilst the basic 5 × 5 game is known as French Crosswords only because it is similar in appearance to crosswords which appear in French newspapers. Its origin is British. Non-competitive word squares have been known since Roman times, the competitive games are late twentieth century inventions. *Countdown* Q-Dye is appearing in print for the first time.

1 AREPO

This name is taken from the classic Latin word square which has been found carved or scratched on stone at Roman sites as far apart as Cirencester, Pompeii and Dura-Europos in Mesopotamia.

```
R O T A S
O P E R A
T E N E T
A R E P O
S A T O R
```

Arepo in this palindromic square is presumed to be a personal name in a translation which reads 'The sower, Arepo, controls the wheels with care'.

Whilst the 5 × 5 square played competitively has the capacity for an individual player to achieve its maximum score of 60 points, it can be safely assumed that a maximum score is impossible with Arepo. The evidence for this assertion comes from considering the results of those who have specialized in constructing word squares. The lower orders of squares (5 × 5, 6 × 6, 7 × 7) have been produced in their hundreds, but the higher orders are almost impossible, though two or three 9 × 9 squares are known. The perfect 10 × 10 is still being sought and the late Dmitri Borgmann has come the closest with his brilliant construction containing weird and wonderful words found in only the most obscure of reference works:

```
O R A N G U T A N G
R A N G A R A N G A
A N D O L A N D O L
N G O T A N G O T A
G A L A N G A L A N
U R A N G U T A N G
T A N G A T A N G A
A N D O L A N D O L
N G O T A N G O T A
G A L A N G A L A N
```

Even using computers, the world's greatest wordsmiths have never managed to equal Borgmann's pencil and paper achievement with its only imperfection the failure to utilize ten different 10-letter words. Attempts at the more difficult square containing 20 different words have failed miserably.

Arepo, in common with the lesser versions, has a bonus score for its word of maximum length. The standard bonus scores for each version in the series are as follows:

5 × 5	A 5-letter word scores 6 points
6 × 6	A 6-letter word scores 7 points
7 × 7	A 7-letter word scores 9 points
8 × 8	An 8-letter word scores 10 points
9 × 9	A 9-letter word scores 12 points

The theoretical maximum scores are:

5 × 5	60 points
6 × 6	84 points
7 × 7	126 points
8 × 8	160 points
9 × 9	216 points

of which only the first two are ever likely to be attained in genuine competitive play, though the 126 points of the 7 × 7 version is not impossible.

Arepo is a perfect contest for the Countdowner. Witness to this is the following match between Ivy Dixon-Baird, a *Countdown* quarter-finalist, and Russell Byers, a finalist. This was their first ever attempt, but it provides standards by which your own efforts may be judged. Match them and you are in distinguished wordsmith company. Ivy lectures in Scrabble at a college of further education and Russell is the current U.K. Scrabble champion. They are also record-breakers in Pears Word Game Society contests.

For their Arepo contest both Ivy and Russell drew 9 × 9 grids and kept their workings secret from each other. They took turns in calling out any letters they wished and both were free to play them within any square on their respective grids. Their completed grids and scores are as follows:

IVY

D	E	S	E	C	R	A	T	E	12
E	A	G	A	H	A	L	A	X	3
M	O	P	C	I	V	A	I	C	3
I	N	S	H	P	I	N	C	H	5
S	H	U	R	M	N	D	V	A	2
T	A	X	D	U	E	M	A	N	3
E	X	P	A	N	D	I	N	G	12
R	I	I	T	K	R	N	E	E	3
S	L	A	P	S	T	E	R	S	5

12 4 3 4 12 6* 4 4 12

---

*Note that Ivy offered RAVINE for this line whereas she could have scored an extra point for the perfectly legitimate RAVINED. Only words offered by a competitor are

In the seventh vertical line Ivy's gamble that LAND-MINE might prove to be an unhyphenated single word failed. Her minor words included AGA, SH, NEE and PIA (it occurs in the *Concise* only as PIA MATER but see the Glossary for the sense in which she knew it as an individual word) and her total score was 109 points.

RUSSELL

P	A	R	A	C	H	U	T	E	12
A	V	E	N	U	E	S	U	S	7
R	E	S	I	L	I	E	N	T	12
A	R	C	D	T	L	R	X	I	3
G	S	I	G	H	D	X	M	M	4
R	A	N	C	H	M	K	I	A	5
A	C	D	N	P	O	I	N	T	5
P	A	E	X	P	A	N	D	E	6
H	E	A	V	I	N	E	S	S	12

12 5 7 2 4 4 4 5 12

Russell emerged as the winner with a total of 121 points and his words are all perfectly normal.

2   COUNTDOWN Q-DYE

Ideally, four people participate in this entertainment, taking turns to switch roles between competitor and official. First, the contest, and again we have Ivy and Russell as the combatants.

The idea is that one player suggests an initial 5-letter word of reasonable flexibility and the other chooses an equally versatile 4-letter word. Once a letter in both words has been changed to create two different words the timing begins and the players attempt to make the highest *Countdown*-style score (i.e. a 9-letter word is worth 18 points, others as normal) out of the resultant nine letters. A full game consists of six double changes.

---

scored but, unlike in *Countdown*, one may (as with Ivy's LAND-MINE) suggest a possible higher-scoring word with a lesser-scoring alternative (LAND or MINE).

In Ivy and Russell's game the initial words were SPEAR and HEAD and the changes, words offered and scores were as follows overleaf.

	Ivy's word/score		Russell's word/score	
SPEAR + HEAD	*		*	
SMEAR + LEAD	SMEARED	7	LEADERS	7
SWEAR + LEND	RENEWALS	8	RENEWALS	8
SWEAT + LENT	WATTLES	7	TALENTS	7
SWEET + TENT	SWEETEN	7	TENETS	0
SWEEP + PENT	SWEETEN	7	SWEETEN	7
STEEP + RENT	PRESENT	7	'PREENEST'	0
		43		29

No sooner had Russell declared 7 for SMEAR + LEAD than he noticed its potential for a 9-letter word. His TENETS scored nil as Ivy's SWEETEN took the honours for the round. 'PREENEST' was merely a desperate gamble as he had already discerned PRESENT, REPENTS and SERPENT and knew that Ivy would score at least 7 points for the final round and, therefore, only a larger word would give him victory.

Before we go any further, can you discern the 9-letter word of SMEAR + LEAD and a better offering than Ivy's winning submission for STEEP + RENT?

Allow yourself 30 seconds per combination.

Between each round of 30 seconds of intense concentration, a light-hearted inquest into the results was made. This proved to be as much fun as any other aspect of the game. A third person, who was the timekeeper, and a fourth who had charge of the dictionary, joined in the discussions.

The full contest consisted of each player being matched in turn with each of the others and it was agreed that this was perfect training for the pressure of competing in the television studio. The aspiring *Countdown* contestant should be fully aware of the tension generated in such an exacting word sport arena if ever he or she faces an audition conducted by the programme's associate producer, Sandra Morgan. It is not enough to be proficient with words and numbers, temperament is also a relevant factor. Four people who organize a *Countdown* Q-Dye session should, if one of their company is on the waiting list for an audition, mirror the show's format as closely as they can.

The words which could have been played in the first and last rounds are EMERALDS from SMEAR + LEAD and PRETENSE from STEEP + RENT.

Peter Newby

Looking at Words

TEMPERAMENTALLY is a rather unique word, though most of us would dismiss it without so much as a second glance. To a wordsmith it is really fascinating. He or she discerns the following:

T	a single-letter word as in **T junction**
EM	A 2-letter word describing the standard unit of measure for the amount of printed matter in a line of type
PER	a 3-letter word, a preposition with a sense of 'through' or 'by'
AMEN	a 4-letter word meaning 'so be it' commonly used at the end of a prayer
TALLY	a 5-letter word having various meanings, one of which is 'score'

and so builds a long word from an ever increasing collection of short words.

One of the secrets of *Countdown* success is to build larger words but the most important thing to recognize is which smaller words have potential and which do not. To illustrate this, note the difference between two dissimilar 4-letter words which might easily occur as the first four letters chosen by a contestant:

(a) | Q | U | I | Z |

No matter what the fifth letter may be, can you think of any possible word which could be produced from QUIZ and that letter?

(b) | D | E | A | L |

Apart from Q, every letter of the alphabet can be added to the constituent letters of this word to produce a 5-letter word. These new words – not all of which are valid for play – are called **andagrams** as they are anagrams of a given word *and* another letter.

A	ALDEA	B	BLADE	C	LACED	D	ADDLE	E	EDALE
F	DALFE	G	GLADE	H	HEALD	I	IDEAL	J	JALED
K	DALEK	L	LADLE	M	MEDAL	N	ELAND	O	ALOED
P	PEDAL	R	ALDER	S	DEALS	T	DELTA	U	LAUDE
V	LAVED	W	WEALD	X	LAXED	Y	DELAY	Z	LAZED

Discounting the group three words:

EDALE (a village in Derbyshire)
DALFE (an obsolete past tense of the verb DELVE)
JALED (an obsolete form of JAILED)
DALEK (in *Chambers* dictionary but it fails to include TARDIS!)
LAUDE (an obsolete form of LAUD)
LAXED (an obsolete adjective meaning 'relaxed')

and the group two words:
ALDEA and ALOED (see Glossary)

the potential is such that a player who can produce only DEAL or any of its anagrams such as DALE, LEAD or LADE is almost certain to lose that round, though the same is not necessarily true of QUIZ.

Now add a fifth letter to DEAL.

D	E	A	L	S

A	ALDEAS	B	BLADES	C	SCALED	D	SADDLE	E	SEALED
F	FALSED	G	GLADES	H	LASHED	I	SAILED	J	?	
K	SLAKED	L	LADLES	M	MEDALS	N	ELANDS	O	ALDOSE
P	PEDALS	R	ALDERS	S	SLADES	T	DELTAS	U	SAULED
V	SLAVED	W	WEALDS	X	?	Y	DELAYS	Z	DAZLES

and there are still exactly the same number (17) of different letters capable of making group one andagrams despite the loss of the J and the X.

Group three words:
FALSED   (an obsolete self-evident adjective)
SAULED   (SAULE is an obsolete verb to satisfy)
DAZLES   (DAZLE is an obsolete form of DAZZLE)

Group two words:
ALDEAS, ALDOSE and SLADES (see Glossary)

The key to potential is the isolation of the flexible letters, so consider the group one words which are the andagrams of a different 5-letter word.

S	T	A	R	E

B	BAREST, BREAST
C	CARETS, CARTES, CASTER, CATERS, CRATES, REACTS, RECAST, TRACES
D	STARED, TRADES, TREADS
E	ARETES, EATERS, SAETER, TEASER
F	AFTERS, FASTER, STRAFE
G	GRATES, STAGER, TARGES
H	EARTHS, HATERS, HEARTS
I	SATIRE, STRIAE, TERAIS
K	SKATER, STRAKE, TAKERS
L	ALERTS, ALTERS, ARTELS, RATELS, SALTER, SLATER, STALER
M	MASTER, MATERS, STREAM, TAMERS
N	ASTERN, STERNA
O	ORATES
P	PATERS, PRATES, REPAST, TAPERS, TRAPES

R	ARREST, RASTER, STARER, TERRAS
S	ASSERT, ASTERS, STARES
T	STATER, TASTER, TATERS, TREATS
V	AVERTS, STARVE, VASTER
W	TAWERS, WASTER, WATERS
X	EXTRAS
Y	STAYER
Z	ERSATZ

The following words would be disallowed for the reasons given:

(a) BASTER, DATERS, SEATER, HASTER, TASKER, LASTER and TAXERS because no such inferable nouns are given in the *Concise*. The same is true of the inferable verbs RESALT, REMAST, RETAPS and RESTAR.

(b) FRATES is defined as foreign.

(c) URATES appears only as the noun URATE in a sense (see Glossary) which makes a plural highly unlikely. Whilst players of all word games attempt to stretch the rules to the limit, the senior editor of the *Concise* assures the writer that she would not permit such a plural for *Countdown*. By contrast, both of the official reference works for Scrabble championships (the British *Official Scrabble Words*[1] and the American *Official Scrabble Players Dictionary*) specifically give URATES, though neither provides a second type of URATE which would make a plural logical. It is controversy of this nature which prompts the House of Waddington to bar plurals from its various word games (Lexicon®, Kan-U-Go® etc.) but which, quite frankly, is a sledgehammer solution for the problem of a comparatively tiny nut.

Common sense should dictate one's attitude towards this particular difficulty and a good rule of thumb is if you can construct a sentence in which a plural is both logical and feasible, then accept

---

[1] See page 31 which discusses the relationship of this book of words to its prime source, *Chambers English Dictionary*.

it. If you cannot, then reject it. Whilst Countdowners have only 30 seconds in which to make a decision, that is an integral aspect of the challenge – gamble, or play safe.

STARE is the basis of no fewer than 71 group one andagrams from the 22 individual letters with which it can be combined – the seeker of superlatives will discover that *Pears Advanced Word-Puzzler's Dictionary* will provide 270! The Countdowner, therefore, who can produce only STARE (or any of its anagrams such as TEARS or RATES) is almost certainly a loser.

Now consider one of the andagrams of STARE.

S	A	T	I	R	E

C	CRISTAE, RACIEST, STEARIC
D	ASTRIDE, DISRATE, STAIDER, TIRADES
E	SERIATE
F	FAIREST
G	GAITERS, STAGIER
H	HASTIER
I	AIRIEST
L	REALIST, RETAILS, SALTIER, SALTIRE
N	NASTIER, RETAINS, RETINAS, RETSINA, STAINER, STEARIN
O	OTARIES
P	PARTIES, PASTIER, PIASTER, PIASTRE, PIRATES, PRATIES, TRAIPSE
R	TARRIES, TARSIER
S	SATIRES
T	ARTIEST, ARTISTE, ATTIRES, IRATEST, TASTIER
V	(VASTIER)
W	WAITERS, WARIEST

More than 60 per cent of the alphabet is capable of providing group one andagrams of SATIRE and you would have to have three highly inflexible letters completing the full *Countdown* set of nine if SATIRE was the best word you could offer. Admittedly, the comparatively flexible A, B and M do not feature in this group one listing but they are well represented in group two and *Pears Advanced Word-Puzzler's Dictionary* raises this total of 41 (possibly 42), given above, to a very substantial 132.

It is important to note that a single A is highly flexible but a second A is not as valuable. SATIRE + A yields three andagrams not quoted above, SATIRE + B yields five and SATIRE + M yields a very impressive ten. To contrast these with other letters SATIRE + N has a magnificent thirty.

When I, the taller of the two writers, submitted my SATIRE research to the senior editor of the *Concise*, Della Thompson, she disallowed two superlatives, ARIDEST and IRATEST, and wrote 'dubious' beside VASTIER. All three are specifically given in both *Official Scrabble Words* and the *Official Scrabble Players Dictionary*. Once again it is a question of logic. 'The most arid' or 'the most irate' are the only forms one would expect to use in standard English but would one use VASTIER or 'the more vasty' in any likely sentence?

VASTY is a rhetorical adjective which owes its modern usage to Shakespeare. It means 'vast' or 'immense' and occurs in *Henry* IV *Part One*:

> 'I can call spirits from the vasty deep'

and in *Henry* V:

> 'The poor souls for whom this hungry war opens his vasty jaws'

All subsequent writers have used the word in a similar fashion and none has made a comparison or suggested an extreme degree of VASTY. Can you honestly see a logical case for the use of the comparative? Della may be small in stature, utterly charming, a delight to the eye, but she can devastate the most arrogant of literary heavyweights and I – at least I am arrogant and overweight – am in awe of this brilliant scholar whose accomplishments include a fluency in Russian! You can rest assured that the famous dictionary corner has the very best instant assessment umpiring of any programme on any broadcasting channel in Britain. When the celebrity guests pay tribute to the various Oxford University Press editors who partner them they are being utterly genuine – even if Gyles Brandreth is a trifle lavish in his praise on occasions. But that's Gyles and he's nobody's fool.

Only one more example of andagramming will be given, that of raising a 7-letter word to an 8-letter word. The significant point is not merely which letters feature but the duplication factor – the difference between one A and two As now that an N has been added to SATIRE, so increasing the size of the basic word. Whereas SATIRE + A has no group one words and only three other words, NASTIER + A has two group one words out of a total of nine possible andagrams. The same is equally true of a duplicated A in the other examples of DEAL + A and STARE + A, an additional A has no group one value whatsoever. Contrast that A with some other letters, and duplication is shown to be an asset. As before, the list is confined to words found in the *Concise*, but if you wish to discover the definitive listing for NASTIER + G see the supreme anagram on page 84.

N	A	S	T	I	E	R

A	ANTISERA, ARTESIAN
B	BANISTER
C	CANISTER, SCANTIER
D	DETRAINS, RANDIEST, STRAINED
E	RESINATE, TRAINEES
G	ANGRIEST, GANISTER, GANTRIES, INGRATES, RANGIEST
I	(INERTIAS), RAINIEST
K	(KERATINS)
L	ENTRAILS, LATRINES, RATLINES, TRENAILS
M	AILMENTS, ALIMENTS, MANLIEST
N	ENTRAINS

O	NOTARIES, NOTARISE
P	PAINTERS, PANTRIES, PERTAINS, PINASTER, REPAINTS
R	RESTRAIN, RETRAINS, STRAINER, TERRAINS, TRAINERS
S	RETSINAS, STRAINERS, (STEARINS)
T	NITRATES, STRAITEN, TERTIANS
U	URINATES
W	(TINWARES)

Della's comments on the bracketed words are as follows:

INERTIAS – not really used in the plural

TINWARES – I would hesitate to allow this

KERATINS/STEARINS – these are particular molecules but use the plural, according to the science editor of the Oxford dictionaries

Whilst extending the study of andagrams up to the *Countdown* maximum of 8 + 1 might prove interesting, the practical limit has now been reached. Statistically, the odds favour the encountering of difficult letters – either in the form of the less flexible or else redundant duplication.

The previous examples of 4 + 1, 5 + 1, 6 + 1 and 7 + 1 illustrate the possibilities which exist when a base word comprising particularly flexible letters is discerned amongst the collection of nine which might occur on *Countdown*. Assuming that one has a reasonable set of letters most contestants can provide a 6-letter word – the winner tends to produce the 7s or, less frequently, the 8s. A sensible study is, therefore, the andagrams of 6-letter words. No answers will be provided but, if you would care to test yourself, you will find that each of the following 6-letter words will provide you with a goodly number of 7-letter andagrams:

> ASTERN, DINERS, GENIAL, GRAINS, INSERT, REGINA, RESAID, RETAIL, SINGER, SLATER, SORTIE, STRIDE and TEASER

Some of these will, at times, lead you to the same word or words. GRAINS + E, REGINA + S and SINGER + A, for example, are identical and *Pears Advanced Word-Puzzler's Dictionary* provides no fewer than 15 words which consist of these same seven letters. To find all or even some is not the object of the exercise, just one will suffice. Each of the above has the potential for combining with a minimum of 50 per cent of the alphabet to provide at least one perfectly valid *Countdown* word, and that is all you need to be a winner.

A by-product of this little investigation – should you decide to pursue it – is that it will turn you from being a Scrabble rabbit into a Scrabble tiger. Any move in this classic board game which has you utilizing all seven of your available letters produces a very high bonus score, so imagine that your available letters consist of ASTERN + Q. The rabbit will play the 6-letter word for a pathetic score, the tiger will miss a turn by changing the Q, knowing that the odds favour the potential for that elusive high-scoring 7-letter word. Tigers on both sides of the Atlantic adopt a similar attitude and if (say) an I has replaced the Q, their eyes light up immediately. The six ASTERN + I words valid for *Countdown* have already been detailed in a previous andagram table.

Not that Scrabble players would in these circumstances discard the Q specifically for the I but for any letter which would prove of value. The player who has a knowledge of the andagram potential of ASTERN is the one who is destined to make a great Scrabble move and, in the process, begin the trail which leads to *Countdown* glory.

Andagrams are normally encountered in crosswords and, for fun, three extreme examples of the compiler's art are given below in the form of partially solved crosswords. The solutions for clues 1 and 2 are words coined by Jeremy Bentham (1748–1832) the famed utilitarian philosopher and writer who also invented the word INTERNATIONAL.

The 18-letter word answer for puzzle number one is the plural of a noun he used in *Chrestomathia*, his 1816 publication of papers on education. The hyphenated 20-letter word answer (it divides as 7–13) for puzzle number two is from his 1818 work, *Church of Englandism and its Catechism Examined*. The clue for this contains a direct quote from that work in which he defines clerics who, by belonging to the school of thought designated by the missing word, are capable of being so described. This 20-letter answer is the longest known non-trival (i.e. fully mixed jumble of letters) andagram.

The 19-letter word answer for puzzle number three is the longest known non-trivial unhyphenated andagram and, like Bentham's words, also found in the *Oxford English Dictionary*. The meanings of the base words (those to which the cryptically described letters are added) are equally genuine but are of no consequence to the understanding of the solutions.

1

Sonoluminescences oddly surround a multiplicity of inferior financial attitudes. (18)

2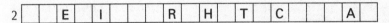

You end amidst strange theoreticopractical description of Bentham's 'pillars of divine wisdom'. (7–13)

3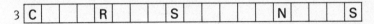

Makes a distinction by way of opposing coadministratrices confused with one centre. (19)

If you enjoy cryptic clues and wish no further assistance then move straight to the final puzzle. But, for many people, they are a complete mystery so an explanation of the format might prove useful:

In puzzle number one, *oddly* is the keyword which tells you that SONOLUMINESCENCES needs to be rearranged so that it will *surround* A. The result of this andagram means 'multiplicity of inferior financial attitudes'.

In puzzle number two, *strange* is the keyword. This time the additional letter is more difficult to decipher. It comes from the *end* of YOU. The meaning is Bentham's metaphor.

In puzzle number three, *confused* is the keyword and the additional letter is in the *centre* of ONE. The meaning is 'makes a distinction by way of opposing'.

To complete this set of four puzzles, a pure anagram. It is not the longest known anagram – this is discussed elsewhere – but an apt description of anagrams, andagrams, antigrams and all other forms of word play of this type.

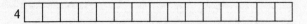

4

Self-descriptive silly pronationalists! (15)

The solutions to all four puzzles are given over the page.

The witty anagrams which John Meade or the former *Countdown* champions in his team, Mark Nyman and Michael Wylie, devise for the Conundrum also have to be 'looked at' in a different way. The trick is *not* to appreciate the humour, otherwise you waste precious seconds before you begin to consider the potential of the nine transposed letters. You should attempt to see them merely as letters, not as a pair of words or whatever other construction has been created to deceive.

Here, for example, is one that would not be chosen as it has a choice of answers:

ONENUDIST

and if this had been based on (say) TENDINOUS then one of the other experts would immediately reject it as it can also be NONSUITED! How would he know this? Not from any anagram book, as none show it, but because he knows how to look at letters and this particular skill is discussed in the following chapter.

Peter Newby

ANSWERS

1 SONOLUMINESCENCES + A = UNECONOMICALNESSES
2 THEORETICOPRACTICAL + U = POETICO-ARCHITECTURAL
3 COADMINISTRATRICES + N = CONTRADISCRIMINATES
4 PRONATIONALISTS = TRANSPOSITIONAL

Short Cuts to Success

The impatient reader will not wish to know the supreme anagram, the concept of andagrams and the fun games which build up a natural expertise with words. He or she will want to rush straight in and score the biggest word possible without bothering with the basics. Can it be done?

Yes. But, without exception, all of the supreme *Countdown* champions have honed their skill with other forms of word play. In the process of playing these games their vocabulary increases naturally as their opponents introduce 'unknown' words which the champions add to their own stockpile of word power. Consider this completed French Crosswords grid. How many points does it score when strictly limited to group one words?

P	S	H	A	W
H	A	P	P	Y
U	D	A	L	N
T	C	R	U	D
S	C	W	M	S

First, the top horizontal line. Does it contain a valid word?

A Scrabble player would recognize immediately a choice between three different interjections: SH, HA or AW. Any one of these perfectly acceptable words would score 2 points for that line. A crossword solver would know HAW, the fruit of the hawthorn, and score 3 points instead. A quiz addict would know SHAW and score 4 points for this archaic word for a thicket.

By contrast, everyone would see HAPPY on the second horizontal line which, being a 5-letter word, has the bonus score of 6 points. Hence your score to date is probably either 9 points (HAW + HAPPY) or 10 points (SHAW + HAPPY). Now score the complete grid, then check your results with the answers given at the end of this chapter.

Admittedly, the 5-letter words are not going to win you many *Countdown* laurels but the game of French Crosswords is delightful and Arepo, the 9-letter version, is a reasonable alternative even though it is far more demanding.

Apart from word power, do the champions have a secret formula for success? Yes. *They consider as few of the letters as possible.* To examine this technique let us play Shelling Peas with the supreme anagram:–

$$\boxed{A}\boxed{E}\boxed{G}\boxed{I}\boxed{N}\boxed{P}\boxed{R}\boxed{S}\boxed{T}$$

(a) The champion will immediately *eliminate* ING and see what he or she can produce with the remainder. We follow the champion's thoughts:

PART.
Add ING.
PARTING.
Is it a noun?
Yes.
Can it be pluralized?
Yes. Add S.
PARTINGS.
(An 8-letter word well within the thirty seconds.)
Still time to spare, what else?

TAPER.
Add ING.
Is it a noun?
Yes.
Can it be pluralized?
Possibly. Add S.
TAPERINGS.
A 9-letter word, but is it safe?
Is there any other possible 9-letter 'ing word'?
REPASTING?

(b) Alternatively, one could first eliminate IER, the comparative ending for an adjective ending in a Y – such as DIRTY to DIRTIER.

> PANS(Y).
> Is it an adjective? Hence, 'PANSIER'?
> I doubt this, so what else is available?
> PAST(Y).
> PASTIER.
> That is a safe enough 7-letter word but what about STAGIER (from STAGY)?
> Still only 7 points. This collection of nine letters is excellent. Am I on the right track?

(c) Or, one could take away IEST, the superlative adjective as DIRTY to DIRTIEST.

> ANGR(Y).
> ANGRIEST.
> RANG(Y).
> RANGIEST.
> Two very safe 8-letter words. Pity about the P.
> Is there such a word as 'PRANGY'?
> 'PRANGIEST'?
> Doubtful, so better to play safe with either 8-letter word.

(d) Or even, IES, the plural of a noun ending in Y as BUNNY with BUNNIES.

> PANTR(Y).
> PANTRIES.
> GANTR(Y).
> GANTRIES.

Now to the dictionary corner where the collective wisdom will match any 8-letter word advanced by a contestant with (say) the remaining group one words of the supreme anagram – GANISTER and INGRATES. However, unless you have already spotted it, the applause will go to the corner for TRAPESING! (TAPERINGS and REPASTING, incidentally, are both group two words and would be disallowed. For TRAPESING see TRAPES in the Glossary.)

If you would now care to test yourself, try the following combinations of letters. In each case you should discern, by taking the attitude of the expert, a 7-letter word almost immediately and may well find a higher scoring word within the 30 seconds you would be given on the programme. To discover what solution will be provided by the dictionary corner see pages 78–83 which introduce the potential of these particular combinations:

AABDEGINR	ADEEIMRST	AEEGNRSST	AEGINRSST
AAEGILNPP	ADEEIMSTT	AEEHIRSTT	AEGINRSTU
ABDGINORS	ADEEINRST	AEEILPRST	AEINNPRST
ABEEILRST	ADEEISSTT	AEEINSTTT	AEINNRRST
ABEEIRRSS	ADEGGINNR	AEEIRSSTT	AEINRSSTT
ACEGILLNR	ADEGINORS	AEFGILNRT	AEIRRSSTT
ACEGILNNS	ADEGINPRV	AEGGINRRT	AGIINRSST
ACEGIMNRT	ADEINORST	AEGHIKNNR	AGILLNOTT
ACEIIMNRT	AEEGILNNT	AEGHILNRS	AGINOPRRT
ACGIMNSTY	AEEGIMNST	AEGHILNRT	AGINORSST
ACGINNOPY	AEEGINNRT	AEGILMNNT	AGINPPRST
ADEEGILNR	AEEGINPRT	AEGINNRTT	
ADEEGINNR	AEEGINRST	AEGINPRSS	

(Note that these combinations have their constituent letters in alphabetical order and that the sequence runs vertically. Thus, the first combination, AABDEGINR, is followed by AAEGILNPP immediately below. This is to mirror the arrangement in which you will discover the solutions. Columnar listing is standard for the dictionary-style listing of this type.)

Peter Newby

ANSWERS

Earlier you were given a French Crosswords target of scoring in excess of 45 points. The example of this chapter does just that. Did you score 46 points?

Horizontal Lines		Vertical Lines	
P S H A W	6	P S W	
H A P P Y	6	H A P P Y	
U D A L	4	U D A L N	
C R U D	4	T R U D	
C W M S	4	S M S	
		6 3 3 4 6	

(Five-letter words score 6 points, all others as number of letters in the word. The Glossary will define PSHAW, UDAL, CWMS, PHUTS and WYNDS.)

Anagrams

Richard Stilgoe is renowned for his love of anagrams. His book, *The Richard Stilgoe Letters*[1], is a delightfully original and witty compilation of short stories about imaginary people whose names are anagrams of his own name. These characters include *Gerald I. Ostrich, Sir Eric Goldhat, Eric Roadlights, Giscard O'Hitler, Dr. Gloria Ethics* and *Doris Lethargic.*

Countdown contestants prize his 'Stilgoeing' of their names far more than the collection of goodies they receive as a consolation for failing to unseat the current champion. These felt-pen-on-cardboard displays of their names – subsequently autographed – are taken home with pride. Even those which are less than flattering (my own name comes out as *Ben ye twerp* or *Bert N. Weepy* in this fashion, though I do not doubt that the master could produce something far more entertaining) are treasured souvenirs of a day in the Yorkshire Television studios.

In July 1989 he quoted on *Countdown* a short verse which had appeared in Geoffrey Smith's *Sunday Times* column just over a year earlier. The verse had first appeared in a book of puzzles published in 1907 and described a year rather neatly:

> JUST A JURY BY NUMBER,
> EACH SCRAP OF YEAR –
> A NUMBER RECORDING
> EVERY JUMBLE, TUMBLE, TEAR.

---

[1]Now available as an Unwin paperback but originally published in 1981 by George Allen and Unwin as a hardback.

The article had stated that this verse was an anagram of all the months of the year but, prior to reading it out, Richard checked it and discovered that this proved false – it was short of five letters. What Richard did *not* reveal to the viewers was the fact that he had to add the remaining letters in a form which rendered the whole thing perfect. Hence, the viewer was given the corrected verse by adding a most apt title to the work.

If you do not wish to discover this for yourself you will find the Richard Stilgoe perfect version at the end of the chapter.

Anagrams have fascinated the literate since the earliest times and they were once considered to be an aspect of magic. Essentially, the significant anagram foretold the future. A famous example concerns the dream of Alexander the Great on the eve of his raising the siege of Tyre. He imagined a satyr dancing round him. His adviser told him that this was a good omen as Σατνρος (the Greek for *satyr*) could be considered as the two words Σα τνρος (*'Tyre is yours'*) and so it proved.

The most profound of all anagrams is the question posed in Latin by Pilate. QUID EST VERITAS? (*'What is truth?'*). This has the unspoken reply of EST VIE QUI ADEST (*'It is the man before you'*).

Even in comparatively modern times a belief in the prophetic aspect of anagrams was held quite seriously and one who was convinced of her prowess in this area was the wife of the poet, Sir John Davies.[2] She annoyed many of her contemporaries with this 'gift' until finally silenced by one who wrote DAME ELEANOR DAVIES, *never so mad a ladie!*

Lewis Carroll had a more gentle touch with his apt anagrams of the famous. His FLORENCE NIGHTINGALE, *flit on, cheering angel* is an oft quoted example, though Richard Stilgoe's FLORENCE NIGHTINGALE anagrams have the same Crimean War connotation but are less eulogistic:

'Fetch Nigel an iron leg'
'Leg on fire? Change lint.'

He even considers her academic qualification for ministering to the wounded. Thus, she possesses 'O' levels in subjects which include:

G.C.E. *Frontline healing*

---

[2] Sir John Davies (1569–1626) was the attorney-general for Ireland from 1606 to 1619.

Personally, I prefer his more ludicrous rearrangements of the lady's name:

> Ringo, the cleaning elf
> Neil, the ginger falcon

are but two of these which add sparkle to the preface of that book of surreal humour based entirely on characters who share the letters of his name.

However, the aptness of an anagram is the standard by which the best rearrangements are traditionally judged:

the aristocracy	a rich Tory caste
HMS Pinafore	name for a ship
punishment	nine thumps
desperation	a rope ends it
endearments	tender names

The above are witty concoctions which the serious student of anagrams would never encounter in wordsmith research. He or she, concerned with the potential of such as ANGERED/ENRAGED for word games, has little time to devote not only to apt anagrams but also to their reverse, the satirical antigrams:

marriage	a grim era
diplomacy	mad policy
mother-in-law	woman Hitler
boardroom	Broadmoor
Margaret Thatcher	that great charmer

These can be equally apt. It depends entirely upon one's viewpoint.

When the *Countdown* contestant Margaret Jones pointed out to Richard Stilgoe that her name had a perfect anagram as *Sergeant Major* she had not created the fun anagram which is the hallmark of the master. A true 'Stilgoe' is a delightfully silly name which aptly describes the character for an imaginary person. PLOD THE SALMON, for instance, is a Welsh policewoman whose duties have her knee-deep in a Glamorgan river guiding the species *Salmo salar*. Plod's efforts being essential for the smooth flow of piscatorial brides and grooms heading upstream to the spawning beds and not being delayed by erstwhile honeymooners returning to a more prosaic lifestyle in the Atlantic Ocean. Plod's real-life counterpart is Della Thompson, who was thus described on one particular edition of *Countdown*!

Creating one's own 'Stilgoes' is great fun and if **stilgoe** follows **clerihew** (see Glossary) into the English language I can guarantee that PLOD THE SALMON will not be an example quoted in the *Concise Oxford Dictionary* as her alter ego is its senior editor!

The truly serious anagrammatists such as the American expert Kyle Corbin, turn their attention to the biggest words they can find and classify them either as trivial or non-trivial according to the degree of letter transposition involved. Trivial anagrams merely transpose a single letter or a syllable whereas the non-trivial are truly amazing discoveries in the field of anagrams. Whilst the trivial yield the longest of all, the non-trivial are far more impressive:

15-letter non-trivial

ANTHROPOMORPHIC	CAPTHORINOMORPH
CINEMATOGRAPHER	MEGACHIROPTERAN
INCONSIDERATION	NONDICTIONARIES
PRETRANSMISSION	TRANSIMPRESSION
PRONATIONALISTS	TRANSPOSITIONAL

16-letter non-trivial

HERMATOCRYSTALLIN   THERMONASTICALLY

17-letter non-trivial

BASIPARACHROMATIN   MARSIPOBRANCHIATA

The trivial anagrams are much easier to discover and include:

21 letters (22 in the plural)
CHROMOPHOTOLITHOGRAPH   PHOTOCHROMOLITHOGRAPH

22 letters (24 in the plural)
CHOLECYSTODUODENOSTOMY DUODENOCHOLECYSTOSTOMY

22 letters (21 in the plural!)
HYDROPNEUMOPERICARDIUM   PNEUMOHYDROPERICARDIUM

This last example is quoted in the *Guinness Book of Records* as being the superlative and we offer a choice between the plural of the CHOLE-/DUODEN- or the single-letter trivial transposition of the 27-letter monsters:

HYDROXYDEOXYCORTICOSTERONES
HYDROXYDESOXYCORTICOSTERONE

as being more worthy of that description.

Speaking of the *Guinness Book of Records* brings to mind the occasion when one of *Countdown*'s celebrity guests quoted its superlative for an English language single-word palindrome, the 9-letter word REDIVIDER which reads the same when read in either direction. The *Oxford English Dictionary* has words that make a nonsense of such a claim. KINNIKINNIK is a mixture used by Red Indians as a substitute for tobacco and its ingredients include dried sumach leaves and the inner bark of willow. This 11-letter word has various spelling forms but the palindromic form is the most oft quoted in view of its intrinsic appeal to word lovers. However, there is one to top even that. The new edition of the OED has a nonce word of James Joyce which it first recorded in its S–Z supplement some years ago. Joyce's TATTARRATTAT (an onomatopoeic equivalent of RAT-A-TAT, the sound of a knock) has no fewer than 12 letters. Incidentally, REDIVIDER is an *inferred* word, it does not appear in *any* dictionary. Much better examples are given in the *Concise*: ROTAVATOR, a machine with rotating blades, and MALAYALAM, a language of southern India. But, I digress. Our subject is anagrams and our concern is with the game of *Countdown*.

Within the last few years an anagram listing formula has been developed whereby the constituent letters of a word are rearranged in alphabetical order, thus the master's surname becomes EGILOST, so, too, is an obsolete word describing one who delivers a laudatory discourse:

EGILOST
elogist
Stilgoe

and, in this fashion, all anagrams can be conveniently indexed under a single heading.

There are a number of books which provide (basically for crossword solving) anagram listings of this type and the American journal *Word Ways* has published a comparison of nine of these. Its table, reproduced below, abbreviates the titles of these books to four letters and it compares their respective results in relation to the 6-letter words known to the magazine's readership as having a minimum of seven different anagrams. Rather than select a particular word and state that it has X number of anagrams the convention is that of alphabetical arrangement of letters and describing its individual words as transposals of those letters. The February 1989 issue of this word players' specialist journal stated the following:

	Pear	Cham	Long	Wett	Hunt	Edwa	Curl	Ball	Haer
ACENRT	9	8	6	5	8	5	8	6	5
ACEPRS	12	4	6	4	9	2	9	7	5
ACERST	12	2	7	2	9	2	9	8	2
AEERST	13	5	3	1	11	3	8	6	3
AEHPRS	14	5	4	3	7	3	7	6	2
AELRST	36	5	9	4	10	2	10	7	3
AEPRSS	12	3	6	2	9	3	8	8	3
EENRST	14	1	4	3	8	1	8	5	1
EINRST	17	3	5	4	7	2	5	5	2
ENORST	11	3	4	1	8	2	7	5	3
EOPRST	18	3	4	2	9	2	6	6	2
	168	42	58	31	95	27	85	69	31

Pears also has 26 transposals of AEPRST *and 25 of* AENRST; *also, the eight-letter group* AEGINRST *has an amazing 23. I unhesitatingly recommend this book for the shelf of any logologist or word-gamesman.*

Unlike the other works, Pears Advanced Word-Puzzler's Dictionary is not an exclusive anagram book, nor is it a pure crossword solving aid. It failed to provide the full listing for the supreme anagram with a 'mere' 23 of the acceptable words of AEGINRST, though this compares very favourably indeed with the other books quoted in the Word Ways table. (These books will be identified shortly but, first, the groupings of letters which constitute the left-hand column.)

If we consider the least impressive letter-group in the above list, ACENRT, it is interesting to see how many of the nine words given in Pears are valid for Countdown. CANTER, CARNET, NECTAR, RECANT, TANREC and TRANCE all pass the test whereas CRETAN has to be disallowed as it is a proper noun. Neither of the remaining two words – the obscure adjective CREANT and the obsolete noun CRANET – features in the Concise, as the last time either of these was recorded in literary use was 1848, which hardly warrants inclusion in a general dictionary for everyday usage.

But, the Countdowner is more concerned with the top-scoring 9-letter words and a sampling of those given in Pears would prove far more useful. The following sample is strictly limited to words valid for *Countdown* and it ignores such as ASPIRANTS/ PARTISANS and ASPIRATES/PARASITES where every combination is a simple plural of 8-letter words.

Essentially this sample is intended to give you an idea of the better combinations of letters which you could find yourself facing in a session of *Countdown* as well as providing excellent ammunition for the *Countdown* training game of Pentery Web discussed on pages 45–47.

But, if you are *not* planning to play Pentery Web (and thereby intend to ignore the 9-letter anagram listing in the interests of fair play) you may care to have a little *Countdown* Conundrum fun instead. The following words are all invalid for *Countdown* but each has at least two anagrams perfectly acceptable for the programme. Can you unscramble at least one for each word?

CARTESIAN, ESTRAPADE, NOCTUIDAE, ITERANCES, CATILINES, SCLEROTIA, ENCURTAIN, CANTINESS, TRICOSANE, OUTRANCES, TOSCANINI, DEFLORATE, RELEADING, MEDIATERS, ARSENIDES, DENTARIES, NEGROIDAL, DRAGONISE, TETANOIDS, LEGANTINE, PIGNERATE, SANGESTER, HETAERIST, GERMANIST, LOAMINESS, MISAUNTER, ASTERIONS, SPINARETS, PARSONETS

To discover the solutions, simply rearrange the constituent letters in alphabetical order e.g. the famous Italian conductor TOSCANINI (1867–1957) becomes ACIINNOST and the dictionary-style indexing reveals a choice of three words all valid for *Countdown*.

A few of the more unusual words in the following list will be defined but these are strictly limited to those unlikely to appear in most of the popular dictionaries, as one cannot assume that the reader possesses the *Concise Oxford*. For example, in the previously mentioned ACENRT group the word TANREC does not feature in such as the *Collins Concise* so it, as well as CREANT and CRANET, will be found in the Glossary.

AABCEELRT	AABDEGINR	AACCIMNOR	AACEGILNS
creatable	bargained	carcinoma	analgesic
traceable	gaberdine	macaronic	angelicas
AABCEILRT	AABDILORT	AACDEEMRT	AACEGLOTU
bacterial	broadtail	demarcate	catalogue
calibrate	tailboard	macerated	coagulate

AACEIMSTT
catamites
masticate

AACEINRST
ascertain
craniates
sectarian

AACENRSSU
anacruses
assurance

AACHIRSST
archaists
catharsis

AACIILRST
racialist
satirical

AADEEPRST
paederast
separated

AADEHLMPS
headlamps
lampshade

AADEIPRST
aspirated
disparate

AADILNOTU
adulation
laudation

AADLORTUY
adulatory
laudatory

AADMNORTY
damnatory
mandatory

AAEGILNOS
analogies
analogise

AAEGILNPP
appealing
lagniappe

AAEILNORT
alienator
rationale

AAGILNOST
analogist
nostalgia

AAIILMPRT
impartial
primatial

AAILLMRTY
maritally
martially

ABDDEIORS
broadside
sideboard

ABDEELNOR
banderole
bandoleer

ABDGINORS
adsorbing
signboard

ABEEGLOPR
bargepole
porbeagle

ABEEHINRT
hibernate
inbreathe

ABEEILRST
beastlier
bleariest
liberates

ABEEILRSV
revisable
verbalise

ABEEILRTV
avertible
veritable

ABEEIRRSS
brasserie
brassiere

ABEIILSST
sibilates
stabilise

ABELNRSTU
subaltern
unstabler

ACCEHIMNS
mechanics
mischance

ACCEHIMST
catechism
schematic

ACCEINORT
accretion
anorectic

ACCEINSTU
encaustic
succinate

ACCELNOVY
concavely
covalency

ACCEORSTU
accouters
accoutres
coruscate

ACDDEEIMT
decimated
medicated

ACDEEILMR
declaimer
reclaimed

ACDEEILNN
celandine
decennial

ACDEELLOT
decollate
ocellated

ACDEIIMRT
diametric
matricide

ACDEILLMY
decimally
medically

ACDEINOTU
auctioned
cautioned
education

ACDHMOOTW
doomwatch
matchwood

ACEEILNRT
interlace
lacertine
reclinate

ACEEINRST
creatines
nectaries

ACEEIRSTU
cauteries
cauterise

ACEELNNRU
cannelure
uncleaner

ACEELNORT
coeternal
tolerance

ACEELNRSS
cleansers
clearness

ACEENNRST
entrances
renascent

ACEGILLNR
cellaring
recalling

ACEGILNNS
cleanings
cleansing

ACEGILRTU
curtilage
graticule

ACEGIMNRT
centigram
cremating

ACEGINRRT
retracing
terracing

ACEHINRRU
hurricane
raunchier

ACEHMORST
chromates
stomacher

ACEIILNST
inelastic
sciential

ACEIIMNRT
criminate
metrician

ACEILLNOR
collinear
coralline

ACEILNOST
coastline
sectional

ACEILNRST
clarinets
larcenist

ACEILORST
loricates
sectorial

ACEILRRTU
recruital
reticular

ACEILRTUV
lucrative
revictual
victualer

ACEIMNRSU
manicures
muscarine

ACEINNORT
container
crenation

ACEINNOS
ascension
canonises

ACEINNRTU
runcinate
uncertain

ACEINNSST
incessant
instances

ACEINORST
creations
narcotise
reactions

ACEINOSST
canoeists
cessation

ACEINRSST
canisters
scenarist

ACENOPRRT
copartner
procreant

ACENORSTU
courtesan
nectarous

ACGHINNST
snatching
stanching

ACGIMNSTY
gymnastic
nystagmic

ACGINNOPY
canopying
poignancy

ACIINNOST
inactions
nicotians
onanistic

ACILLOPTY
optically
topically

ACILLOSTY
callosity
stoically

ACILMNOPT
complaint
compliant

ACIMNORST
narcotism
romantics

ACINNORST
constrain
transonic

ADDEEENRS
deadeners
serenaded

ADDEEGLNR
gladdener
glandered

ADDEEMNRU
maundered
undreamed

ADDEERRSS
addresser
readdress

ADDEGIMNN
demanding
maddening

ADEEEGLRT
regelated
relegated

ADEEENRTV
enervated
venerated

ADEEFLORT
floreated
refloated

ADEEGILNR
engrailed
realigned

ADEEGINNR
endearing
engrained
grenadine

ADEEIMRST
diameters
dreamiest

ADEEIMSTT
estimated
meditates

ADEEINPRT
pertained
repainted

ADEEINRSS
nearsides
readiness

ADEEINRST
detainers
resinated

ADEEISSTT
stateside
steadiest

ADEELNRTU
unaltered
unrelated

ADEEMNOUR
demeanour
enamoured

ADEEPRSTU
depasture
depurates

ADEGGINNR
deranging
gandering
gardening

ADEGILNOR
girandole
reloading

ADEGINORS
grandiose
organdies
organised

ADEGINPRT
departing
predating

ADEGINPRV
depraving
pervading

ADEIMORST
amortised
mediators

ADEINNSTU
inundates
unstained

ADEINORST
derations
notarised
ordinates

ADEINOSTT
antidotes
stationed

ADEOPRRTY
portrayed
predatory

ADFLORRWY
forwardly
frowardly

AEEFMNORS
forenames
freemason

AEEGILLRS
allergies
galleries

AEEGILNNT
eglantine
inelegant

AEEGIMNST
geminates
magnetise

AEEGINNRT
argentine
tangerine

AEEGINPRT
interpage
repeating

AEEGINRST
reseating
stingaree

AEEGNRSST
estranges
greatness
sergeants

AEEGOPRRT
porterage
reportage

AEEHIRSTT
earthiest
heartiest
hesitater

AEEILMNNT
alinement
lineament

AEEILPRST
pearliest
prelatise

AEEILRSTV
relatives
versatile

AEEINSTTT
intestate
satinette

AEEINTTTV
attentive
tentative

AEEIRSSTT
sestertia
treatises

AEELMNPSS
ampleness
ensamples

AEELPRRST
palterers
plasterer

AEELSSSTT
stateless
tasteless

AEEMNSTTT
statement
testament

AEENNPRTT
penetrant
repentant

AEEOPRSTT
operettas
poetaster

AEFGILNRT
faltering
reflating

AEFHINORS
fashioner
refashion

AEGGINRRT
gartering
regrating

AEGHIKNNR
hankering
harkening

AEGHILNRS
narghiles
shearling

AEGHILNRT
earthling
haltering
lathering

AEGILMNNT
alignment
lamenting

AEGILNPRY
parleying
replaying

AEGIMNRST
emigrants
mastering
streaming

AEGIMNRSU
geraniums
measuring

AEGINNRTT
integrant
nattering

AEGINPRSS
aspersing
repassing

AEGINRSST
asserting
ganisters

AEGINRSTU
gauntries
signature

AEIINNRSS
raininess
sirenians

AEILMNOSS
loaminess
melanosis

AEILMSTTU
mutilates
stimulate
ultimates

AEILNPRTY
interplay
painterly

AEILNSSST
saltiness
stainless

AEIMNRSTU
antiserum
ruminates

AEINNORTV
nervation
vernation

AEINNRSTT
instanter
transient

AEINNRSTY
tyrannies
tyrannise

AEINORSST
assertion
notarises
senoritas

AEINNPRST
terrapins
transpire

AEINPRSST
paintress
pinasters

AEINNRRST
restrains
strainers
tarriness
transires

AEINRSSTT
resistant
straitens

AEIRRSSTT
starriest
traitress

AELLORSWW
swallower
wallowers

AENOPRSST
patroness
transpose

AGHILMORT
algorithm
logarithm

AGHMNOOPR
monograph
phonogram

AGIINRSTT
straiting
striating

AGILLNOTT
allotting
totalling

AGINOPRRT
parroting
prorating

AGINORSST	AGMMNOORS	AIINORTTT	AILNOORST
assorting	groomsman	attrition	tonsorial
organists	monograms	titration	torsonial
roastings			

AGINPPRST	AIINNORTU	AIIOPRSTT	AILORSUVY
strapping	ruination	parotitis	savourily
trappings	urination	topiarist	variously

The above sampling of *Countdown*-valid words taken from *Pears Advanced Word-Puzzler's Dictionary* has been limited by virtue of space to those anagrams which, alphabetically transposed, are indexed with the letter A. *Pears* has transposals up to:

IINORSTTU
introitus
routinist

though the ultimate *Countdown*-valid indexing would be:

GINOPRSTU
posturing
sprouting

This system of indexing is now used by most of the works concerned with the recording of anagrams and was first mentioned in the book *Mathematical Carnival* (Alfred A. Knopf Inc., 1975), where the credit is given to one Nicholas Temperley. The author, Martin Gardner, discussed Temperley's concept for an anagram dictionary as a crossword-solving tool and his original idea has now become an established fact. One of Gardner's own examples has a crossword clue of THE CLASSROOM which, transposed as ACEHMOORSST, gives the very apt solution of SCHOOLMASTER.

However, of the anagram dictionaries quoted in the *Word Ways* table I have been able to identify all except the one abbreviated as 'Haer' and most of the remainder use Temperley's system of indexing. Those which do not ('Hunt', 'Curl' and 'Ball') constantly repeat themselves as, for example, with a word such as CATER. CATER would reveal that its anagrams are CRATE and TRACE. CRATE would have CATER and TRACE and, similarly, TRACE would have CATER and CRATE.

Now imagine how much space would be required under the pre-Temperley system to cope with such as the words of the supreme anagram. If one accepts all of Borgmann's *sensible* discoveries including such as trade names and historical personages such as ST REGINA, we have no fewer than 47 transposals of the letters AEGINRST. This would involve 47 separate entries each containing 46 different words. But, even ignoring superlatives such as this, an 'old-fashioned' anagram dictionary has to be at least twice as big as it need be. The identified dictionaries together with their totals for the supreme anagram are as follows:

'Pear'	*Pears Advanced Word-Puzzler's Dictionary*	23
'Cham'	*Chambers Anagrams*	2
'Long'	*Longman's Anagram Dictionary*	4
'Wett'	*The Word Game Winning Dictionary* (Bruce Wetterau)	2
'Hunt'	*The Dictionary of Anagrams* (Samuel Hunter)	7
'Edwa'	*The Crossword Anagram Dictionary* (R. J. Edwards)	1
'Curl'	*The Anagram Dictionary* (Michael Curl)	8
'Ball'	*The Nuttall Dictionary of Anagrams* (A. R. Ball)	10

Pears uses the Temperley system though, ironically, the best of the others ('Hunt', 'Curl' and 'Ball') have the prodigal 'old-fashioned' system. The solitary word which 'Edwa' has for the supreme anagram is GANISTER and this is found in the book that proudly boasts on its cover that 'It will solve *any* anagram within seconds' ... at least Edwards improved on his total of one when he found three others for his subsequent *Longman's Anagram Dictionary*!

Obviously, the Borgmann research was not known to any of the compilers of the above works and, therefore, it is hardly surprising that *The Guinness Book of Records* which, until the advent of *Pears*, used to quote the 34 known anagrams of ASTER as being the supreme anagram. With 36 transposals of AELRST, *Pears* has established an unimpeachable world record for the supreme recorded anagram which title it still holds until the definitive listing for AEGINRST is given. *The Complete Countdown Companion* cannot be construed as an authority and it will be interesting to see which will be the first work of substance to make the definitive pronouncement on the supreme anagram. Strict guidelines need to be drawn and, once established, perhaps *Guinness* will revive the category and give full credit not only to Borgmann but also his co-researchers including *Countdown's* Darryl Francis.

A delightful by-product of the Temperley system of indexing is that one can discover all manner of trivia – such as, what is the ultimate 9-letter word comprising letters strictly limited to the second half of the alphabet? PROTOZOON (NOOOOPRTZ) is a typical example, and the ultimate word in the *Concise* would appear to be TORTUROUS (OORRSTTUU). However, an alternative spelling of TOPSYTURVY, the rare UPSYTURVY (PRSTUUVYY) would seem to be the ultimate in any dictionary.

Finally, the solution to the amazing verse which caught Richard Stilgoe's eye in the *Sunday Times* but which has five letters unaccounted for. The trick is to provide a title from the letters A, E, O, M and P.

The master's answer is simply A POEM!

Peter Newby

Countdown Crosswords

These are six unique crosswords to test your *Countdown* skills.

For each crossword clue, merely select from the given letters those which are needed for its answer. All clues have nine letters but only a 9-letter word answer will utilize all of them. It should be noted that the *Concise* has been plundered to find some of its more obscure offerings. These obscure words are highlighted by reference to the Glossary. For example, in the first crossword you are told that 6 across has an unusual word. The given letters of AHHHKKNXY could provide ANKH, HANK or KHAN. If you think that it could be one of these and it is relatively uncommon, is that word in the Glossary? If it is, then you have solved that particular clue.

The solutions for the crosswords are on pages 92–94.

CROSSWORD 1

Across

1	AAGINORTV	(9)
5	BBLNNNOYZ	(5)
6	AHHHKKNXY	(4)
7	EGGMMPPPY	(4)
8	HHIMMSTXZ	(5)
9	BDEIISSUZ	(9)

Down

1	AANORRRST	(9)
2	CEHIIMOSS	(9)
3	AABDEEGNT	(9)
4	ABEEIPRTZ	(9)

The meanings of the crossword answers for clues 6 across, 7 across and 2 down will be found in the Glossary.

CROSSWORD 2

Across

  1 BEEHNOOPX (9)
  6 AADDFFMNO (5)
  7 CEERSWXYZ (5)
  8 AADHILLRS (9)
  9 AEILNOPRT (9)
  12 FGHILMNNY (5)
  13 GILLNORST (5)
  14 ADGGLRSSU (9)

Down

  2 HMNPPRRYZ (5)
  3 ADEGILLNP (9)
  4 EEEOOORRR (5)
  5 ACDEORSST (5.4)
  6 AALLNRTUY (9)
  7 AGIILNORS (9)
  10 AEGILNRST (5)
  11 EEEGGGRRR (5)

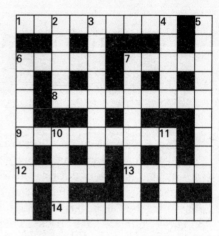

The meanings of the crossword answers for clues 1 across, 8 across, 9 across and 11 down will be found in the Glossary.

CROSSWORD 3

Across
  1 CDNNOOTUW (9)
  6 AAAGHNTYY (8)
  7 AAAILSVXY (6)
  8 DEGIKNRRS (8)
 10 EOOORSWXZ (6)
 13 AAALRSTWY (6)
 15 ACDEIOPST (8)
 16 CDEHILLYZ (6)
 17 AACDEEIMT (8)
 18 DEEGINNTX (9)

Down
  1 CDOORRSSW (9)
  2 CEINOSVWY (6)
  3 ADDRSWXYZ (6)
  4 AEENNRSSS (8)
  5 ACEEHIKRV (8)
  9 AACGLLSWY (9)
 11 AEGORSTTU (8)
 12 EHILOQRTY (8)
 13 AACCDDEES (6)
 14 DEINNTTTW (6)

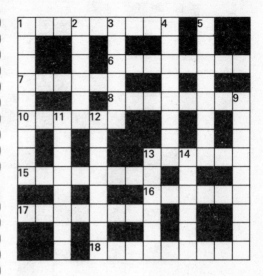

The meanings of the crossword answers for clues 6 across, 3 down and 12 down will be found in the Glossary.

CROSSWORD 4

Across

- 3 BEEGHIRTY   (9)
- 7 EINOOQUXY   (7)
- 8 AIINOPRTT   (9)
- 9 DDEIPSTUY   (7)
- 10 DEIIOSXYZ   (6)
- 11 AADIINORT   (9)
- 13 ELOPQSSUZ   (6)
- 16 DDDEELPYY   (6)
- 18 EEELMNOPT   (9)
- 21 EEEFFLTTT   (6)
- 22 AAACEHSST   (7)
- 23 INOOPSTTU   (9)
- 24 DEINNSWXY   (7)
- 25 DEHHLOOSU   (9)

Down

- 1 EILQRRSUV   (8)
- 2 BCIIINUUX   (6)
- 3 EEEPRTXYZ   (6)
- 4 BBDENOTTU   (8)
- 5 EGIINQRTU   (8)
- 6 AINRSTTYY   (8)
- 12 GIIILOOOP   (5)
- 13 FHHOORSTV   (8)
- 14 ALPPSTUYY   (8)
- 15 EEHHIPPSS   (8)
- 17 ADEILTTTU   (8)
- 19 AAADEPPSS   (6)
- 20 AAACCMSWW   (6)

The meanings of the crossword answers for clues 3 across, 2 down, 6 down, 13 down and 20 down will be found in the Glossary.

CROSSWORD 5

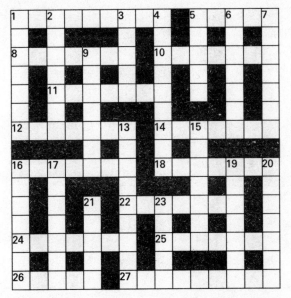

Across

1 ACEGIMTUZ (9)
5 BBBCCCEEX (5)
8 AEGINPRST (7)
10 BBGGIILLN (7)
11 AABBILORT (7)
12 AEGGINRSS (7)
14 ACELLTTXY (7)
16 CDEENORTU (7)
18 DEIIOVXYZ (7)
22 EMNORTUVW (7)
24 BBIKTUXYZ (7)
25 CEEHOORRR (7)
26 BBBHRRSUU (5)
27 ADDNORSWW (9)

Down

1 EHPRSWXYZ (7)
2 CINNORTUV (7)
3 AAOORRTTZ (5)
4 AABCELLOR (9)
5 ELMUVWXYZ (5)
6 BBEIKKRST (7)
7 CCEGGNOOY (7)
9 AABBELTUX (7)
13 ADEIIRSTZ (9)
15 AAHHIMTUZ (7)
16 EEKKOORSV (7)
17 BBCCELORZ (7)
19 EEIINNRRT (7)
20 EEPPPRSTX (7)
21 AAABBQSUU (5)
23 AACCMMWWX (5)

The meanings of the crossword answers for clues 1 across, 5 across, 18 across, 24 across, 1 down, 4 down, 5 down, 15 down and 23 down will be found in the Glossary.

CROSSWORD 6

Across

3	ACEENRRTU	(7)	
8	ADEILNOPP	(5)	
9	BCDHIJYZZ	(5)	
10	IILMSTUVW	(7)	
11	CCOOPPUUY	(5)	
12	FFIILLXYZ	(5)	
13	AIIILLLPP	(7)	
14	ACDDEINST	(5)	
16	AACCRRXYZ	(5)	
18	ADEEIISSS	(7)	
21	GGGMMMOSS	(4)	

22	EEEGGGYYY	(4)
23	AEHISTXYZ	(7)
26	CCIINNOOZ	(5)
28	AALLRRVVY	(5)
31	AAEILLXYZ	(7)
32	AEGILNRST	(5)
33	AACCIITTY	(5)
34	CCEEIITTZ	(7)
35	AABBIILLY	(5)
36	AALLMMVVW	(5)
37	EEKKNQSTU	(7)

Down

1	ACDINRRRR	(6)	19	AAADDDQUZ	(3)
2	AAADEJPSY	(6)	20	DEIUVWWWW	(3)
3	ELLRRSSTU	(7)	23	AGHINOTWZ	(7)
4	AEGIMNRST	(7)	24	EIIIILNRS	(7)
5	CCDEEFFII	(7)	25	AACCEELRT	(7)
6	AAAELWXYZ	(6)	26	AAAIIGGZZ	(6)
7	AGGHSYYYZ	(6)	27	CCCEIOONT	(6)
15	AABBIIMMY	(5)	29	AAEHHLLTT	(6)
17	AGLLLQUYZ	(5)	30	AACCSUUYY	(6)

The meanings of the crossword answers for clues 10 across, 11 across, 13 across, 26 across, 31 across, 34 across, 37 across, 6 down, 7 down, 15 down, 17 down, 19 down, 20 down, 23 down, 24 down, 27 down and 30 down will be found in the Glossary.

ANSWERS

1

2

3

4

5

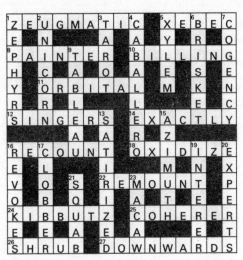

6

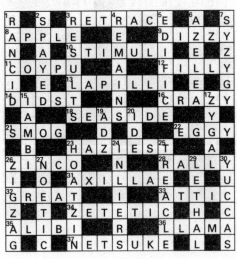

(*Left*) The most
famous chairman
since Mao –
Richard Whiteley.

(*Right*) Beauty as well as
brains – Carol Vorderman.

(*Above*) Two *Countdown* stalwarts – Richard Stilgoe and Gyles Brandreth.

(*Right*) Bill Tidy looking a picture with hostess Kathy Hytner and Carol Vorderman.

(*Above*) Richard and Gyles with the young maestro – Allan Saldanha.

(*Left*) Gyles with a book he actually hasn't written.

(*Left*) Actress Sylvia
Syms.

(*Right*) Bill and Gyles
togged up for the 500th
Countdown.

(Right) A youthful looking Ned Sherrin.

(Below) London taxi-drivers' favourite, Nigel Rees.

(*Above*) Patrick Mower with Carol and Kathy.

(*Opposite, above*) Nita Marr (*seated*) with (*standing, left to right*) Derek Nimmo, Kathy, Richard, lexicographer Catherine Clarke and Carol.

(*Opposite, below*) Dublin's fair city produced wonder-boy Tim Morrissey flanked by (*left to right*) Richard, Carol, Lance Percival, lexicographer Georgia Hole and hostess Lucy Summers.

(A*bove*) 'The harmless drudges', lexicographer Della Thompson and Peter Newby.

(*Right*) The shorter of the two authors, John Meade, *Countdown* series producer.

Those Who Dwell
in Dictionary Dell

Richard Stilgoe's anagram of my name – Joe Hedman – is obviously quite appropriate but I often wish I wasn't the 'headman' when I receive hundreds of letters from viewers complaining about my choice of celebrity 'to dwell in dictionary dell' with the lexicographer. Indeed, many write to ask why we need one anyway. Get rid of the waffle they say, so we can have more games.

However high the standard of our contestants, the chances are that viewers at home can occasionally beat them, as indeed do our guests on the show. I feel it is my duty to provide the longest possible word to stop viewers writing or phoning to say they've beaten the contestants. (If anyone does write to say they have beaten our contestants *and* experts we immediately send an application form by return of post!) And remember our guests in Dictionary Corner have a tremendous advantage. They have longer to find a word and they have a lexicographer with a dictionary next to them.

When I first employed Oxford University Press the lexicographers expressed concern that they might be forced to make hurried decisions because they were on television where timing was of paramount importance. I told them they could take as much time as they wanted. Any interminable delay I could shorten in editing or the celebrities could help pass the time by providing their words or suitable anecdotes. Words are great fun and it's my feeling that the banter between Richard and the celebrities celebrates the beauty of our language whilst providing some welcome light relief. If we can provide education through entertainment, even better.

How do I choose my celebrities? First and foremost they must have credibility. The late Eric Morecambe was a brilliant man but I doubt if the viewers would have believed him if he had come up with long words on *Countdown*.

I insist on meeting anyone who wishes to join our team. We make up to six shows a day so it's imperative that, under pressure, we can all still smile and get on with it. No tantrums, please!

Our guests must all have their own gimmick; their own identity. Richard Stilgoe was an obvious choice as we've already learned, so was Bill Tidy with his cartoons. In the old days I would have expected Lance Percival to offer all his words in calypso form, but he doesn't do that any more, so we had to come up with something else. Let Lance explain:

'The first time I met John Meade he was holed up in a hotel suite interviewing prospective guests for *Countdown*. I was late, he was shutting up shop, but the little devil was delighted to open up again and show me tapes of the show. He explained what was required with great enthusiasm; I nodded my head with crawling sagacity. He asked me if I had any ideas about what I would do on the show as a guest, I tried to look bemused and asked him if that was a trick question. He thought trick questions were a great idea, I nodded with even more crawling sagacity... of such stuff is showbiz history written.

Ever since then he has done the nodding and I have scoured the length and breadth of Britain for trick questions! You want an example? Well you're getting one anyway... THERE IS THREE ERRERS IN THIS.' (*Solution on page* 103 *at the end of this chapter.*)

One man who didn't need a gimmick was the late Kenneth Williams. He was brilliant, but such hard work. Before each recording date he would ask me to prepare a 'crib sheet', listing the definitions and etymology of hundreds of words. If one of those words, or a synonym, cropped up, Kenny (off camera) would glance at his list, and then when the cameras were on him he would eruditely define it. Cheating? No. Professionalism, especially when he'd top his explanation with a brilliant anecdote.

You could never switch Kenny off. Outside the studio, during lunch or dinner, he would regale us, irrespective of gender, with the filthiest limericks known to man!

It was Kenny who recommended Gyles Brandreth to me and over the years he has proved hard work for a different reason. Out of three dozen or so celebrities we've used on *Countdown* he attracts the most mail. You don't just like Gyles. Viewers love him or hate him; in fact, I think, judging from the letters a lot of people love to hate him. But one thing's for sure, you can't ignore him. It's not just his jumpers that provide colour to the proceedings. He might come across as a clown but behind that persona lies a very shrewd and remarkable talent, and believe me his enthusiasm is infectious.

We tend to record *Countdown* in three or four day blocks and come the last day we're all, understandably, wilting. For this reason I've always tried to book Gyles for the final sessions. As soon as he arrives his personality and boundless energy lifts us all, especially as he's always got a new challenge up one of his gaudy sleeves. I've managed to top him only once during the years I've worked with him. Gyles was proud to have had the world's shortest poem published with his *Ode to a Goldfish*, which goes simply 'Oh wet pet'. I managed to beat him with *My debt to Snow White by the Seven Dwarves*. It goes: 'I O I O'!

Within a year or so *Countdown* had become a cult programme. Personalities, who genuinely enjoyed playing the game at home, would approach me via their agents. After appearing on a show, what never failed to surprise them was the reaction of 'the man in the street'. John Junkin, another regular contributor, told me that in his many years in show business he had never worked on a show which resulted in his receiving so much attention whilst going about his everyday business. Nigel Rees takes up the theme:

'I have to say that of all the programmes I have ever been associated with, I have never known one with the kind of audience that *Countdown* has. I sometimes think that even if I wrote a novel like *War and Peace*, when I died the obits would say, "OCCASIONAL CONTRIBUTOR TO COUNTDOWN DIES". I have had taxi-drivers scream to a halt in London to tell me that they watch, there is a newspaper-seller at Oxford Circus who never fails to ask me when I'm next going to be on; and, above all, it is very difficult to walk into a hotel or restaurant without porters and waiters getting wildly excited (even if English is definitely not their first language).

When asked how they manage to catch *Countdown* at 4.30 in the afternoon, taxi-drivers, newspaper vendors and my shoe-mender, admit that they tape it. Some even seem to watch it in the middle of the night. As for hotel porters and waiters – I think 4.30 must be a very slack time in their working lives, and that's why they watch it. On one occasion I was walking through Shepherds Market in Mayfair and was warmly greeted by two ladies of the night, and not for the obvious reason. It seems that *Countdown* is on at a slack time for them, too . . .

Apart from which, of course, vast armies of the retired come in from the garden for their tea as *Countdown* begins and seem to make up a very sizeable slice of the audience. They are quite fanatical about the show.

Perhaps the most difficult part of being in Dictionary Corner is not sounding superior when one is able to come up with a longer word than the competitors. I suppose that is why the TV listings person in the *Independent* once told readers: "The smart Alec in Dictionary Corner today is Nigel Rees" (in fact, it was Eve Pollard, but no matter).

Compensation comes in the form of the letters that come in response to things one has said. Never slow to point out one's errors (though politely), the *Countdown* viewer is also wonderfully helpful. When I raised the topic of collective nouns (and discovered, to my surprise, that there were people all over the country obsessed with the subject), I received some delicious suggestions. Amongst those aired were: a BRAY of vicars; a TROUSER of ferrets; a COMMENTARY of "arlotts"; a WINCE of dentists and a RINSE of dental patients; and a HANDFUL of bras.

When I talked of words for various phobias, one viewer (who enjoys inventing them) wrote: "It is with a certain measure of diffidence that I have written to you, as you may feel threatened by THAUMASTONEPISTOLOPHOBIA (a fear of receiving fan-mail)." Another drew my attention to an interesting "philia": a GYNOTIKOLOBOMASOPHILE, he said, is apparently someone who enjoys nibbling a woman's ear-lobe.

When I raised the subject of pet-names for household objects, we heard about: a house called LAUTREC because it has two loos; a Hoover called J EDGAR; a car called FLATTERY, because it will get you anywhere, and a wok called HEREWARD THE WOK.

In early appearances I made something of the resemblance between myself and Richard Whiteley (we have been genuinely mistaken for each other, though always to Richard's advantage). When I was discussing middle names, however, I did manage to reveal to an astonished nation that "Richard" is, in fact, his middle name rather than his first name, which is "John". He is, therefore, in fact "JR" Whiteley – which hardly needs pointing out, I suppose!

Finally, as I am supposed to be the quotations expert may I supply one for *Countdown*? Adapting what Thomas Hughes said of cricket in *Tom Brown's Schooldays*, *Countdown* is "more than a game – it's an institution" and long may it remain so!'

Sylvia Syms should be so lucky. She wrote to me thus:

'No matter how clever I thought myself nobody wrote to say *that*! They simply wanted to know three things. Was I ever in love with my leading men? Is Joan Sims my sister? Where did I buy my blouses?'

As for another of our 'Thespian' guests, Simon Williams, he wasn't really sure how to take one compliment he received from a lady whilst waiting in the post office: 'I used to think you were just an actor but now I've seen you on *Countdown* I can see that you're a person as well!'

I contracted Simon, along with Brian Johnston, Sally James and Patrick Mower, following their appearances in another show of mine, *Ask No Questions*, presented by John Junkin and Carol Vorderman (who else?). They discovered that *Countdown* was under my wing and asked me if they might have a go.

Tim Rice came to my notice by accident. I was listening to a radio programme on which three celebrities, including Tim, were bemoaning the declining standards of British television. Then Tim said that the only programme he really enjoyed was *Countdown*. I was on to his agent the next day.

As I mentioned earlier I do insist on having lunch or at least meeting with any potential *Countdown* celebrity first. (I refused to book a very well-established female broadcaster because her agent told me she couldn't spare the time for a meeting!) But one person whom I did contract without first getting to know was Derek Nimmo. A few days before we were due in studio a celebrity gave back word – his agent had double-booked him and he had to honour the first contract. Sandra phoned around all the agencies to see if any of our regular celebrities could step into the breach. None was available, but one agent did say he was sure that Derek Nimmo, 'who absolutely loves *Countdown*', would like to do it. He was abroad at the time but if we gave the agent recording details he would make sure Derek was there.

Sure enough on the morning of the recording Derek arrived, immaculate as ever, sun-tanned (yes, it is hyphenated) and raring to go. There was one slight problem. He'd never actually seen the programme! A quick crash course followed, and Nimmo, the ultimate professional, produced the goods and the words. Whether the agent had been 'trying it on' or he'd made a genuine mistake didn't matter. Derek is now a regular member of the club!

Sir Clement Freud was suggested to me by Paul Fox, at that time our Managing Director. They'd met at a cocktail party in London and the former Liberal MP had indicated that he might be interested in appearing on *Countdown*. I subsequently arranged to meet him in the bar of a hotel in Mayfair.

Sir Clement duly arrived at the appointed time and after a couple of minutes of gentle banter we began talking 'shop'. Automatically I reached for a cigarette.

'I hope you're not going to smoke that?' he asked in such a way that brooked no argument. Well, I thought, I can last an hour or so without a cigarette, so we continued to chat amicably about *Countdown*. He could actually do the numbers game, he said. It was only after he'd illustrated his numerical prowess a few times that I realized he kept using the same numbers which, as all Countdowners know, is not allowed. When I pointed this out to him he smiled boyishly and professed that he thought they shouldn't be that easy.

By now I was ready for a cigarette but Sir Clement showed no signs of preparing to leave. Was he simply captivated by my company? No. He eventually told me that Yorkshire Television cameras were filming his London flat for the *Through the Keyhole* series and he couldn't return home for a few hours. Before or since I've never gone as long without a cigarette! Sir Clement is another regular contributor to *Countdown* and, as long as I don't smoke in his company, I'm allowed to call him by his sobriquet, Clay.

The late Russell Harty was without doubt one of my favourite people. Russell had taught young master Whiteley at Giggleswick and over the years they'd become friends, Russell living in Giggleswick and Richard having a cottage in nearby Masham. Richard mentioned that Russell might be interested in appearing; he certainly watched the show. We fixed up lunch and it was there, at the Devonshire Arms in Bolton Abbey, that I observed an amazing thing. Seconds after we sat down at the table, Richard, subconsciously perhaps, assumed a pupil role as Russell held forth.

We decided that Richard and Russell should 'adopt' the teacher–pupil relationship on *Countdown*. It worked brilliantly.

Dinah Sheridan is a true fan of *Countdown*. She writes:

'I don't usually watch television in the afternoon, but I am devoted to words and word games, so noticing it announced in my newspaper I did switch on for the very first edition of *Countdown*. (All the while ignorant of the fact that it is like "crack" – unfortunately immediately and totally addictive, also destructive.)

My life revolves around the programme. I used to enjoy having friends in for tea: no longer!

The telephone is off the hook and this has, for all I know, cost me professional engagements and therefore tragic loss of income. I don't care if it busts me – I love it!'

I first met Dinah at our studios whilst she was filming *The Flying Lady*. Dinah had been stood down for a couple of hours and she asked if it was possible to sit in whilst we recorded *Countdown*, as it was her favourite programme. Of course I agreed. So Dinah's first appearance on *Countdown* was as a member of the studio audience!

The only other celebrity I would like to mention in some detail is Carol Thatcher. I had liked Carol seconds after first meeting her for lunch in London and signed her up straight away. Before she arrived on the studio floor I warned all the production crews, and particularly our 'warm up' man, Graham Thornton, against cracking any political jokes; she was here as Carol Thatcher, writer and broadcaster, not Carol Thatcher, daughter of that 'Great Charmer'. So what happens? In the first programme she came up with the word **tricorn**, which she said was a cocked hat, with the brim turned up on three sides. 'The type of silly hat mummy's always wearing,' she said. In the next game a contestant offered **navigate**. 'Ah,' she said, 'Brother Mark wouldn't know that word would he?', alluding to his rally driving exploits! She had the audience eating out of her hands after that.

On one occasion, after the day's recordings we were all going out for dinner. Carol and I waited in the club bar whilst Richard brought his car around to the front. About half an hour elapsed before a flummoxed Richard arrived on foot to say he'd called the police as he'd locked his keys in the car with the engine still running. Totally unphased, Carol acquired a wire coat hanger, broke into Richard's car, and returned to finish her drink!

Finally, I would like to mention one person who only appeared in 'Dictionary Dell' for two games. Ned Sherrin was booked but we were about to start recording and he'd not arrived. A call to his home was answered by the man himself. He'd got his dates mixed up, he apologized, but he'd catch the first train to Leeds. All well and good. My problem was that I had a studio booked and a studio audience waiting for action. I was pondering what to do when I had a brainwave. I looked at the hapless Mark Nyman and told him I was going to make him a star. Just you come up with the long words, I told him. 'What about the jokes?' he cried. 'Don't worry,' I assured him. What I did was put him on 'key producer talk-back'. I shouted puns down the ear piece, Mark came up with the words, Richard coaxed him along, and the result was Mark enjoyed himself so much that he was somewhat miffed when Ned eventually turned up.

I always promised Ned that I'd get my own back for his lateness on that day and now, through Carol Vorderman, I can. Carol reports:

'One day we were recording *Countdown* in the Yorkshire Television studios in Leeds with Ned Sherrin as the guest celebrity in Dictionary Corner. As we were walking out of the studio at the end of one of the programmes I started chatting to Ned about *Ziegfield*, a show which had recently opened in the West End. I was going on about the disappointing reviews and how unkind the critics had been. Ned turned to me and said, "Well, it will be interesting to see what Tommy Steele does to the production" (Tommy Steele had just been brought in as the director). I said, "Yes, he certainly can't do any worse than they've done already. By the way, Ned, have you seen it yet?" Ned turned to me with his 6'3" frame, looked me straight in the eye and said "Yes darling, I wrote it."'

The celebrities who have dwelt in 'Dictionary Dell' over the years at the time of going to press are:

Barbara Taylor Bradford
Gyles Brandreth
Ken Bruce
William Davies
Liz Frazer
Sir Clement Freud
Russell Harty
Frazer Hines
Sally James
Martin Jarvis
Brian Johnston
John Junkin
Rula Lenska
Ted Moult
Patrick Mower
Derek Nimmo

Lee Peck
Lance Percival
Eve Pollard
Nigel Rees
Tim Rice
Ann Robinson
Willie Rushton
Dinah Sheridan
Ned Sherrin
Diane Solomon
Richard Stilgoe
Sylvia Syms
Carol Thatcher
Bill Tidy
Kenneth Williams
Ernie Wise

Solution to Percival's Poser: The third error is that there are only two errors!

John Meade

The Contestants

At the end of the day it doesn't matter how well I do my job, what form Richard is in, or who's in Dictionary Corner, the success of *Countdown* is totally dependent on the contestants. The buck stops with Sandra Morgan, my Researcher for the past five years, now Associate Producer.

It's Sandra who travels regularly to Aberdeen, Birmingham, Bristol, Cardiff, Derby, Edinburgh, Leeds, London, Manchester, Newcastle, Portsmouth, Southampton, Dublin, and occasionally Jersey, to interview contestants. In the early days Sandra used to advertise for contestants in the national press. As the show is now so successful viewers write direct to the production office and all are invited to an interview. There, they are given a test which consists of six letters games, three numbers games, and six conundrums.

From those results contestants are selected, and to an extent seeded. But what has to be remembered is that it can be as long as a year before a chosen contestant actually ends up in the studio. During that intervening period they might not have played *Countdown* as much, and no one can gauge how they will react once the cameras are rolling.

Read what chartered accountant Mick Keeble, a beaten finalist, has to say:

'It was obvious that the television studio affected people to a different extent. Strangely enough, although I was very tense at first, I relaxed completely after having had the word **spooked** disallowed, presumably because the worst thing that can happen to a contestant on *Countdown* is having what he or she considers is a perfectly good word disallowed. In a later game, though, the nerves returned and, picking up my glass for a drink, I had to quickly return it to the table as my hand was shaking so much. Needless to say, my dry mouth immediately became much worse, and so the only remedy was to slide the glass towards me and, hoping the camera didn't return to me too soon, bend down to the desk and, using both hands, manage to take a furtive sip. So although I felt mentally OK I was at times a physical wreck.'

Eddie Murphy, another successful contestant, nearly didn't even make the studios:

'On the big day I was a bag of nerves travelling to Leeds, and kept saying to myself, what on earth have I let myself in for? Here I was, an ex-foundry worker, who, because of illness, left school at 13 years of age! Shall I turn back?'

Robert Richland, losing semi-finalist in Series Four, agonizes: 'I never admitted being nervous whilst in the studio, but after every programme that I was on, I had to rush to the nearest loo to relieve myself. So adrenalin wasn't the only thing flowing in abundance.'

As I've already mentioned we record at least five shows a day, often six, and sometimes seven or eight! In between shows we have a 'turn around' of about 15 minutes, so a successful contestant doesn't get much chance to relax. Even lunch doesn't offer much respite. Robert Richland again: 'After a 51–51 draw against Stuart Schofield we had to *endure* the buffet break before our re-match. Needless to say I wasn't very hungry.'

I remember some years ago a contestant from Edinburgh who, to be honest, was getting on everybody's nerves with his brashness. What he wasn't going to do when he got on the show was nobody's business! His test score was indeed very impressive, but what happened?

In the first round of the game he declared nothing, and despite some humane coaxing by Richard his total score after nine rounds was just 5!

Many is the time that Sandra will confidently predict that the next contestant will win 'at least' five games only to see him or her beaten out of sight in the first game. We do our best to relax them. Part of Mark and Michael's job as production team members is to meet and greet all contestants at the hotel the night before recording. They advise them, rehearse with them, make sure that the taxis are ordered to get them to the studios on time – molly-coddle them in fact. But at the end of the day no one can predict how they'll react once the red light goes on.

My last word on this subject will be a classic example of 'bottling'. As you know, Michael Wylie is one of the finest Countdowners to emerge over the years. He's been part of the production team for seven years, and yet when he took to the floor again last year for the *Breakfast Countdown Masters* he totally blew the first three rounds. Fortunately for Michael we had a technical problem and we had to re-record and he went on to win his match very comfortably.

Michael was one of our early contestants and, apart from his brilliance at the numbers game, he was also an exception in another sense – he wasn't a Scrabble player. Most of the successful players during the years are top class Scrabblers – Mark Nyman, Russell Byers, Harvey Freeman, Ash Haji, Darryl Francis, Bill Bradford, Alan Simmons, Joyce Cansfield, Richard Evans and so on. Of course it's not surprising. Words are such an important part of their lives, though in the early days we often heard the moan go out, following a disallowed word, 'Well, it's in *Chambers*!' Canny Scrabble players have succeeded on *Countdown* by deciding not to offer a word they know exists but in all probability would not be listed in the *Concise*. Here's Bill Bradford:

> 'In my first round of the play-offs I was lucky enough to see the word **kohlrabi** which no one in the studio believed except Ned Sherrin who knew it was a vegetable.
>
> In the semi-final I was defeated mainly due to my word **hooley** being disallowed in the Dictionary Corner because it was not in the *Concise*, though Ned, like me, knew it was a party usually held in Ireland. Having said this I believe that the *Concise Oxford* should remain the arbiter, because too many obscure words would make the programme too highbrow and lose its appeal to its many admirers.'

Thank you Bill!

In retrospect, contestants in the earlier series, and especially Scrabble players, had it harder, as words not listed were often allowed by the lexicographers. They would use their own judgement and claim a certain word was allowable 'because it's in common usage'. That ruling would have been all well and good if we'd had the luxury of having the same lexicographer adjudicating all the time but unfortunately for us that's not possible. So the problem arose that one lexicographer would deem a word acceptable but another wouldn't.

Darryl Francis remembers having the word **gabbier** disallowed. 'In those days no one had formulated any rules about allowing comparatives and superlatives. Kenneth Williams intoned that **gabbier** wasn't in the dictionary so couldn't possibly be allowed.' (As **gabby** is listed in the *Concise* the comparative would now be allowed.)

In the end I held a meeting in Oxford with all the lexicographers and after a good deal of discussion it was decided that any word not listed simply would not be allowed, eliminating the problem, specifically, of 'er' words. Now I feel we've just about got it right, though plurals of scientific words can sometimes cause headaches for the lexicographer.

Occasionally mistakes can be made, of course. The classic one just had to involve the precocious phenomenon, Allan Saldanha, who had the word **yolked** disallowed in the final of Series 16. Julia Swannel, a brilliant lexicographer, had simply misread the dictionary. Allan lost by 11 points to Dick Green. Viewers were sympathetic then outraged when it was discovered **yolked** was indeed listed in the *Concise*. *Countdown* received its greatest publicity ever, headlines in all the 'pop' papers. Julia admitted her mistake and though I pointed out that Allan would have still lost by 5 points if **yolked** had been allowed, I accepted that he might have been affected psychologically. The problem was solved when I decided to give Allan the complete leather bound set of *Oxford* dictionaries worth £2,000!

I'm actually proud of the way we treat our contestants. We put them up in decent hotels, they are wined and dined once the recordings are over. Many have become good friends. In eight years we've only had one complaint from a contestant who wrongly claimed 'he was robbed', when a word was disallowed.

I'll let the contestant Nita Marr, who shares Richard's birthday, give her views:

Remembering *Countdown*

Happy memories of *Countdown* still remain with me today.
As I send you this greeting on our 'Umpty-Fourth' birthday.
When I recall those words and numbers the memories that stick
are of sometimes feeling brilliant and sometimes feeling thick!
When you've been a *Countdown* champion you acquire a touch of
fame.
And folk you've never met are quite familiar with your name.
I bumped into a lady in an Edinburgh loo.
She said 'Saw you on *Countdown*, rooted every day for you.'
It's nice to see so many folks are fans of this great show.
I've made new friends because of it, you will be pleased to know.
And finally I knew that even though I didn't win,
I was still the sole contestant who was Richard Whiteley's twin!

Having learned something about the backgrounds of our more
successful contestants, it's not too surprising to learn that the
majority of the most unusual words that have emerged on *Countdown*
over the years have been proffered by those who regularly play
Scrabble at the highest level or who have studied at least one
specialist subject.

On the other hand the majority of words disallowed by *Countdown*'s
legion of lexicographers were suggested by that same strata of
contestants, disproving the maxim that a *little* knowledge is a
dangerous thing!

As we have learned words ending in 'er', 'ier' and 'iest' are often
not specified in the *Concise* though they may be reasonably deemed
by any right-thinking member of the community as being in common
English usage. The same applies to 'un' and 're' words and, of
course, possible hyphenated words. So, although *Countdown* is
obviously a game requiring a great deal of skill, fortune can favour
the brave gambler.

In the final of Series 17 Evan Simpson offered the word **eloigns**.
He actually knew that it was a legal expression, but the fact that the
Shorter Oxford proved him correct was little compensation to him as
it wasn't entered in the *Concise*! (Evan had been 7 points down
against Lawrence Pearse, the eventual champion, and had felt he
had to gamble to stay in with a chance.)

The time for players to gamble is, of course, when they are so far behind that they're practically in a no-win situation, or when they're so far ahead that they can afford a disallowed word. It can also depend on who Richard Whiteley speaks to first. For example Player A may have a certain 8-letter word and a dubious 9-letter word. If Richard asks Player A first how many letters are in his word, he's likely to plump for the safe 8. If, however, Richard asks Player B first and he says 9, then Player A will obviously go for his dubious 9.

The players might look relaxed 'on screen' but remember they just have 30 seconds to see the word and then a couple of seconds to make up their minds on what they'll offer. Pressure indeed!

Taking all these points into consideration, I've perused the files covering all the televized *Countdown* games and come up with what, in my opinion, are the best words to score over the years. As Mark Nyman is a member of the production team, he has obviously played more *Countdown* games by far than any contestants, therefore, the majority of the words listed are his. Modesty forbids this writer to include any of his own attempts. Although my 'exclusive' 9-letter word, **Vindaloos**, curried no favour with the lexicographer!

Here is the list, with definitions (if needed) in the Glossary:

Mark Nyman	Other Contestants	
CAVETTO	**Andrew Munday**	NECKTIE
FORESTAYS	**John Widdowson**	MEWLING
AGOUTIS	**Clive Spate**	TREFOILS
INWEAVE	**Richard Evans**	NONAGES
ORTOLANS	**Peter Evans**	EPINASTY
GATEPOST	**David White**	ZEUGMA
ANSERINE	**David Trace**	CLAVIERS
PARLANCES	**Robert Richland**	BEZIQUE
AMBULENT	**Mike Willis**	BROLLIES
ANGELUS	"	BEAUTS
TERRAPINS	"	QUALITY
EPIBLAST	"	BETIMES
GROMMET	**Les Martin**	POLENTAS
VIRAGOS	**William Bradford**	KOHLRABI
PARODISTS	**Michael Wylie**	PINNACES
BIRDCAGE	"	BEATNIKS
LORIMERS	**Derek Rutter**	CANGUES

TETRAGON	**John Wallace**	UNLATCHES
TRAVOIS	"	WATERLOGS
VIRELAYS	**Ian Bebbington**	MOPPET
RAGSTONE	**Tim O Kane**	MOIDERS
WAHINES	**Darryl Francis**	ZIRCON
SOUTANES	"	RAVELINS
AMBUENT	"	NIELLO
VESICATE	**Olivia Lloyd Potts**	PROXIES
PURSLANE	**Harvey Freeman**	REARMOST
VORTICES	"	URAEMIA
PRONATED	"	ANTHERS
ECLOGUES	"	PIGTAILS
DIURETICS	"	TRAGEDIAN
DARIOLES	**Dick Green**	GRANTEES
MODESTER	**Nic Brown**	LIONETS
MATZO	"	TRELLISES
THALWEG	**S. Williams/B. Owen**	SWANLIKE
DUENNAS	**Steve Williams**	SALIENTS
CAROTENES	**Evan Simpson**	CALCITES
PHONATES	**Lawrence Pearse**	BLOOPERS
GALIPOTS	"	CAPRINE
HETAIRA	**Tony Vick**	TORQUES
GUNBOATS	**Allan Saldanha**	EDUCATOR
BEDTIMES	**Frank Clark**	VALANCES

John Meade

Coinage

One of the most memorable moments in the whole of *Countdown* was the offering by 12-year-old Tim Morrissey of Dublin of the possible word STEAKED in his semi-final of series 17. When asked to define it he said, 'A cow that has been murdered'.

Unfortunately, the word does not exist, but the delightful humour of this genre has been in existence for many years and *Pears Word Games* uses the term sportmanteaux to describe the deliberate constructions of non-serious portmanteau words which blend the sound and sense and combine the meanings of two words. Whilst Tim's STEAKED is not a true portmanteau word such as OXBRIDGE (a combination of OXford and CamBRIDGE) it does approximate to sportmanteaux words such as these:

AMSTERDAMP   a type of Dutch smog
BELFASTEROIDS   inter-community communications freely exchanged in Ulster's capital city in times of trouble

Any subject can be utilized in this fashion and one can have fun defining a VORDERMANIAC or describing a person who is BRANDRETHERAL rather than BRADFORDINARY, as is a different writer in the dictionary corner. Who could possibly be WHITELIER than Whiteley or even the RICEST of the lot? Is Sylvia a SYMSTRESS and what comes out of Carol's THATCHERY on a FREUDAY? Could it be SHERRINGS? Do the BILLITERATE suffer from TIDYSLEXIA and has Richard STILGONE for yet another unique name? Does Della write THOMPSONNETS or Dinah perform a SHERIDANCE? Is the PERCIVALUE of a JOHNSTONIC HINESTIMABLE? And what is Eve's POLLARDUOUSNESS?

A sportmanteau word requires a definition in order to be humorous, but an allied form, the qwaint, is complete in itself and very popular with advertising agencies. *Countdown* champion Darryl Francis has had a number of his qwaints published and among his gems are:

Decembrrr, twogether, HUMiLiTY, neverendin

Some qwaints have even appeared in the *Oxford English Dictionary*. It records, under LISP, the jocular LITHP and its plural LITHPH. Qwaint is a particularly apt choice of name for these constructions which have been defined in the prestigious American journal of recreational linguistics, *Word Ways*, as 'ingeniously designed, self-descriptive, word-like letter-sequences possessing the quality of the words suggested'. This revival of a Middle English spelling of QUAINT not only looks quaint but returns the sense of 'ingeniously designed' to the word itself. QUAINT, in the days when it was spelt with a W, had that additional meaning.

'QW words' still exist and one of very recent coinage is due to appear in the 1990 *Concise*. The existing ones – now found only in various dialects – are QWAT, QWINE, QWIRK, QWOP and QWOT. These, which are recorded only in specialist dictionaries, are defined in the Glossary, whilst QWAINT – as a modern fun noun – has yet to be noted by a lexicographer though it has a sufficient currency to warrant this. There are a number of 'non-U Q words' and it will be nice to see the *Concise* validating another of these, QWERTY, for *Countdown*.

QUAINT's lost meaning as 'ingeniously designed' is not unique, as many of our words gradually change their sense. In the previous paragraph, for instance, I used the word NICE – but, in what sense? Over the centuries it has drifted from meaning ignorant, to foolish, to over-scrupulous, to precise, to pleasant and even today there are some who insist that it still means precise and reject its meaning pleasant.

The co-editors of the new edition of the *Oxford English Dictionary*, Edmund Weiner and John Simpson, have been quoted in a press article[1] as concluding that the English language is getting bigger. But, they admit it may simply be that more of it is visible owing to the democratization of the printed media. Classical models are going out and new word forms tend to have more English bases. Scientists do still use Greek and Latin roots for new words, but they usually get them wrong. Spelling, which reached a fairly standard level 50 years ago, is now becoming inconsistent again, not by becoming more logical but through the carelessness of writers and publishers.

Be that as it may, we are in safe hands with the *Concise*, though if Gyles Brandreth had his way, we would also pay attention to his favourite dictionary, a satirical masterpiece given a high profile in his own superb masterwork *The Joy of Lex*.

The Joy of Lex[2] has a complete chapter devoted to the genius of Ambrose Gwinnet Bierce and a sampling from Bierce's *The Devil's Dictionary*[3] will explain Gyles's enthusiasm for this American wit and man of action who, in 1913, set off for Mexico (then in the midst of a revolution) and was never seen again.

These examples provide a fitting climax to this chapter as they are yet a third version of humorous word coinage. This time we know the word, but the definition is something else! (Tim Morrissey, you have joined an exclusive band of praiseworthy neologists. Your wit is worthy of recording alongside that of Bierce, the greatest of all of the language's funsters.) For pure verbal ambrosia enjoy the following:

absurdity *n* A statement of belief manifestly inconsistent with one's own opinion.

accordian *n* An instrument in harmony with the sentiments of an assassin.

alone *adj* In bad company.

bore *n* A person who talks when you wish him to listen.

clairvoyant *n* A person, commonly a woman, who has the power of seeing that which is invisible to her patron – namely, that he is a blockhead.

---

[1] Issue 28 of *The Independent Magazine* (March 1989).

[2] First published in 1980 by William Morrow & Company Inc., New York.

[3] Now available as *The Enlarged Devil's Dictionary* in the Penguin Classics series with many of Bierce's original definitions rediscovered from their original sources. The 1989 film *Old Gringo* has Gregory Peck as the eponymous hero, Bierce.

congratulation *n* The civility of envy.

déjeuner *n* The breakfast of an American who has been in Paris. Variously pronounced.

diplomacy *n* The patriotic art of lying for one's country.

egotist *n* A person of low taste, more interested in himself than in me.

fashion *n* A despot whom the wise ridicule and obey.

happiness *n* An agreeable sensation arising from contemplating the misery of another.

ivory *n* A substance kindly provided by nature for making billiard balls. It is usually harvested from the mouths of elephants.
(Taken from the E*nlarged* edition, see Footnote 3.)

jury *n* A number of persons appointed by a court to assist the attorneys in preventing law from degenerating into justice.

> Against all law and evidence,
>   The prisoner was acquitted.
> The judge exclaimed: 'Is common sense
>   To jurors not permitted?'
> The prisoner's counsel rose and bowed:
>   'Your honor why this fury?
> By law the judge is not allowed
>   To sit upon a jury.'

(Also from the E*nlarged* edition.)

Finally, and what could be so apt?

lexicographer *n* A pestilent fellow who, under the pretense of recording some particular stage in the development of a language, does what he can to arrest its growth, stiffen its flexibility and mechanize its methods. For your lexicographer, having written his dictionary, comes to be considered as 'one having authority', whereas his function is only to make a record, not to give a law. The natural servility of the human understanding having invested him with judicial power, surrenders its right of reason and submits itself to a chronicle as if it were a statute. Let the dictionary (for example) mark a good word as 'obsolete' or 'obsolescent' and few men thereafter venture to use it, whatever their need of it and however desirable its restoration to favor – whereby the process of impoverishment is accelerated and speech decays. On the contrary, the bold and discerning writer who, recognizing the truth that language must grow by innovation if it is to grow at all, makes new words and uses the old in an unfamiliar sense, has no following and is tartly reminded that 'it isn't in the dictionary' – although down to the time of the first lexicographer (Heaven forgive him!) no author ever had used a word that *was* in the dictionary. In the golden prime and high noon of English speech; when from the lips of the great Elizabethans fell words that made their own meaning and carried it in their very sound; when a Shakespeare and a Bacon were possible, and the language now rapidly perishing at one end and slowly renewed at the other was in vigorous growth and hardy preservation – sweeter than honey and stronger than a lion – the lexicographer was a person unknown, the dictionary a creation which his Creator had not created him to create.

Hell *n* The residence of the late Dr. Noah Webster, dictionary-maker.

Peter Newby

The Vital Statistician

Carol Vorderman writes:

'2 November 1982 is a date engraved on my memory, not only because it's the date when Channel 4 was launched and I became the first girl to be seen on it, but because of the chaos when my family and I gathered to watch the momentous occasion. My boyfriend had brought along a bottle of vintage champagne to launch Channel 4 and when I went to take it from the fridge, the bottle slipped and smashed on the kitchen floor. My mum and I had hired a video recorder especially to tape the programme and ten minutes before the start the machine broke down. My brother Anton had come up from London to celebrate the event, he settled down on the floor in front of the telly, his foot caught the table and knocked it over, breaking bottles and glasses.'

An appropriate way, I think, to launch a smashing career in television.

As I mentioned in the chapter relating to the history of *Countdown*, our statistician in the regional series failed to get one numbers game right when the contestants failed. In those days we could offer little help, although now most of us in the production team have become pretty adept in this aspect of the game (yes, we all play along in the production gallery, even after all these years).

So my first priority when Channel 4 commissioned Yorkshire Television was to find a replacement. Ideally I wanted an attractive girl to make my play on words 'vital statistician' have some meaning. I advertised in the national press and was inundated with applications from professors, computer experts, mathematicians and, to be honest, more than a few ladies who 'were willing to do anything to get into television'. Ignoring the last category, I travelled the length and breadth of the country, interviewing and testing. I discounted 75 per cent of interviewees straight away as they were lost without a calculator. The remainder I had to ignore because they just wouldn't 'look good' on screen. Eventually, I met Dr. Linda Barrett from Manchester. She fitted the bill, but alas there was a problem. Her professional commitments meant that she might not be able to make all the recording dates. But at least Dr. Barrett could attend the initial recordings, so I contracted her.

I confessed my problem to a friend of mine, Jim Greenfield, the show business correspondent of the *Yorkshire Evening Post*. Within a couple of days news of my plight was headlined on the front page of the newspaper. The next day I received a hand-delivered envelope from a Mrs. Jean Vorderman. It included a photograph of her 21-year-old daughter Carol who had just attained a First Class Honours Degree in Engineering at Cambridge University. Carol was living with her mum in Headingley, Leeds, not ten minutes away from the Y.T.V. studios. An interview was hastily arranged. Every maths problem I threw at her, she solved. Yes, she was available.

Now I had two vital statisticians, so during the first series I decided to use them as a team. When one of them was 'on screen', the other would also work out the solution 'off screen'. I selected Carol to appear on the first show.

When the clock began counting down during her first ever numbers game, I noticed on an 'off air' monitor, Carol put down her pen after five seconds. Was it an easy one? Neither contestant could do it. 'What about you, Carol?' inquired Richard. 'Yes,' said Carol and proceeded to stun the studio and television audience with her numerical skills. Frank Smith led the applause in the gallery.

During that first series I continued to alternate between Dr. Barrett and Carol. Both were excellent statisticians, but with no disrespect to Linda, it was Carol who had what I call the 'X' factor.

One day Carol approached me to say that she had a difficult choice to make. At the time she was working for a computer company, taking days off to accommodate *Countdown*. She just could not continue to do both jobs. Did I think she had the talent to make television her full-time career? 'Yes,' I replied, without hesitation, and if she promised to make *Countdown* her priority whatever other television opportunities came along, I would help her start her new profession by making her the sole statistician. Linda departed and Carol went from strength to strength.

Now, of course, Carol is rarely off our screens, but her commitment to *Countdown* remains; so much so, that last year I felt her 'X' factor was being wasted on the numbers section alone, so I asked her if she'd have a go at the selection of letters. She agreed, 'As long as you don't call me a hostess!' Would we dare?

The statistician's role was vital in those early days. My assumption that we were a more literate than numerate nation was proved correct many times over, and Carol had to illustrate her skills at least once during every programme.

In the first series there was one notable exception. Michael Wylie, a genial, shy, portly youngster from Edinburgh, amazed us all with his calculations. In the five preliminary rounds that he won, Michael scored maximum points from the numbers games. (Michael lost in the semi-finals to the eventual champion Joyce Cansfield.)

When we first met Michael he was unemployed, but his previous job was working in a bookmakers. Hence, his mental mathematical ability! I am pleased to say that Michael is now a valued member of my production team, and to prove his talents are not exclusive to numeracy, he's a budding children's author to boot!

Michael apart, the general standard of numeracy was low, but such is the high quality of contestants now, only 'all-rounders' can seriously aspire to the championship. What has been very evident in the past is that if *Countdown* is off our screens, future contestants do not practise the numbers game at home in readiness for their recording sessions. As Sandra Morgan, my Researcher and Associate Producer says: 'When we are recording future *Countdowns* whilst previously recorded shows are being transmitted, the standard is very high. But if we are "off-air" whilst we are making future shows, the performance regarding the numbers games drops. Obviously, most contestants only practise their numbers games by watching *Countdown*. If it's not on, they don't seem to bother.'

In the following chapters Peter Newby proves that numbers can be fun.

John Meade

Bringing Numbers into Play

Many people confess to being either good with the words aspect of *Countdown* or with the mathematical side, but not with both. The supreme example of this type of selective ability has to be Jedediah Buxton (1707–1772) who lived at Elmton near Clowne, Derbyshire.

Jedediah Buxton, the son of the village schoolmaster, was completely illiterate but his mathematical genius was such that he was invited to London to demonstrate his abilities before the Royal Society. When they asked him what was the product of a farthing doubled 139 times he gave the result not only in pounds sterling but then multiplied this enormous number by itself. Now a celebrity, he was taken to see Garrick's performance as Richard III but paid no attention to the action of the play. Instead, he amused himself by counting the number of words spoken by the great actor.

A more practical use of his talents was made by Jedediah's local squire, Sir John de Rhodes, who wished to know the exact size of his estate, Barlborough Hall. Jedediah gave him the answer first in acres, rods and perches; then in square inches; finally in hairsbreadths!

No matter which way one inclines, whether it be to words or numbers, there are one or two little amusements which can induce an interest in the less favoured skill. These combine words and numbers, and the mastery of the techniques involved should result in an all-round *Countdown* performer – even Jedediah Buxton might have become a man of letters had he ever been introduced to one of the following two hybrids.

1   CRYPTARITHMETIC

The classic hybrid. This combines word wit and simple mathematical ability. You set yourself the task of saying something which is either very apt or very ironic and which statement is capable of unique mathematical proof. For an apt example consider the fact that two odds always make an even. Written arithmetically it is shown thus:

$$
\begin{array}{r}
O\ D\ D \\
O\ D\ D\ + \\
\hline
E\ V\ E\ N
\end{array}
$$

Can this be proved mathematically? Just as significant, is the answer unique?

This puzzle contains five different letters each of which (algebra-style) represents a different numeral. What combination of numerals would make sense?

First of all, the E *must* represent one. No other digit is mathematically possible. So we begin our solution by writing a one wherever the letter E occurs:

$$
\begin{array}{r}
.\ \ .\ \ . \\
.\ \ .\ \ .\ + \\
\hline
1\ \ .\ \ 1\ \ .
\end{array}
$$

To produce the one in the tens position of the answer can only be achieved by making D equal to five:

$$
\begin{array}{r}
.\ \ 5\ \ 5 \\
.\ \ 5\ \ 5\ + \\
\hline
1\ \ .\ \ 1\ \ 0
\end{array}
$$

Sadly, there are now two possible solutions:

$$
\begin{array}{r}
8\ \ 5\ \ 5 \\
8\ \ 5\ \ 5\ + \\
\hline
1\ 7\ 1\ 0
\end{array}
\qquad\qquad
\begin{array}{r}
6\ \ 5\ \ 5 \\
6\ \ 5\ \ 5\ + \\
\hline
1\ 3\ 1\ 0
\end{array}
$$

So it fails the test of a unique solution.

Creating witty cryptarithmetic puzzles is quite a challenge and perfect ones are worthy of publication as teasers for others to solve. Here are two of mine – one apt, the other ironic – which have been published elsewhere but both fall into the perfect category as each has a unique solution:

(1)	N I N E	(2)	W R O N G
	N I N E		W R O N G +
	N I N E +		R I G H T
	H E L P		

Whilst researching the *Concise* for this book, I chanced upon the curious plural AREG discussed elsewhere. This struck me as being ideal for a cryptarithmetic puzzle so I experimented with various numbers of its singular, ERG, until I found that four is perfect:

(3)
E R G
E R G
E R G
E R G +

A R E G

But, a neat paradox – also making its first appearance in print – concerns the fact that NEAT is both singular and plural and means either OX or OXEN in the sense of one (or more than one) of the bovine kind. However, 4a and 4b have different solutions. Which of these is perfect?

(4a)	N E A T	(4b)	O X E N
	N E A T		O X E N
	N E A T +		O X E N +
	O X E N		N E A T

Any mathematical symbols can be utilized for cryptarithmetic purposes and different mathematical challenges can be just as tantalizing as those of simple addition. With subtraction, for example, one can make equally amusing statements. But, can one create a perfect teaser?

In an attempt to produce an original one for this book which would be a little more profound than most, I tried with:

$$\begin{array}{r} A\ D\ A\ M \\ R\ I\ B\ - \\ \hline E\ V\ E \end{array}$$

but failed to produce a single mathematical solution. However, by changing the lady's name:

$$\begin{array}{r} A\ D\ A\ M \\ R\ I\ B\ - \\ \hline E\ V\ A \end{array}$$

there were solutions galore. Here are some:

$$\begin{array}{r} 1\ 0\ 1\ 5 \\ 3\ 2\ 4\ - \\ \hline 6\ 9\ 1 \end{array} \qquad \begin{array}{r} 1\ 0\ 1\ 6 \\ 7\ 3\ 5\ - \\ \hline 2\ 8\ 1 \end{array} \qquad \begin{array}{r} 1\ 0\ 1\ 7 \\ 5\ 9\ 6\ - \\ \hline 4\ 2\ 1 \end{array} \qquad \begin{array}{r} 1\ 0\ 1\ 8 \\ 4\ 2\ 7\ - \\ \hline 5\ 9\ 1 \end{array} \qquad \begin{array}{r} 1\ 0\ 1\ 9 \\ 2\ 5\ 8\ - \\ \hline 7\ 6\ 1 \end{array}$$

Finally, I devised one which is very apt and, ironically, the most difficult to solve:

$$\begin{array}{r} (5)\quad B\ R\ A\ Z\ I\ L \\ T\ R\ E\ E\ S\quad - \\ \hline D\ E\ S\ E\ R\ T \end{array}$$

The solutions to these puzzles are given at the end of this chapter, on page 128, but, if you wish to construct your own, you could see what happens if you allow RABBITS to multiply or have a HOUSE divided. Does any plant have a square root worthy of comment? The best known of the hybrids is limited only by your imagination and skill.

Cryptarithmetic puzzles have appeared in various publications, but they have one very serious drawback, their scope is very restricted. Only ten letters may be considered at any one time and the production of the perfect puzzle is bedevilled by the fact that many otherwise clever statements are confounded by a multiplicity of solutions. Similar limitation applies to most other hybrids which, in the main, are based on alphapositional values so that A always represents 1, B equals 2, and continue through the alphabet culminating with Z as 26. Some of these are very clever but the end result is always the same, only the experts can produce anything worthwhile.

This is not the case with Sumwords. Its competitive applications were explored fully in *Pears Word Games* (in which the concept was first published), but much of what follows is appearing in print for the first time and revolves around the words and numbers skills of Countdowners.

2 SUMWORDS

The letter B occurs, on average, once in every hundred letters of standard English prose. So, too, do the letters G and V. By contrast, those same hundred letters will include 13 Es, 9 Ts and 4 Ds but J, K, Q, X and Z will, in all probability, be completely absent. Assigning individual letter-values which reflect a realistic view of their frequency of use in the language and including decimal points up to .5 we have the following table:

A 8.5	F 3	K 0.5	P 3.1	U 3.3
B 1.5	G 1.3	L 4.5	Q 0.4	V 1
C 3.5	H 6	M 2.5	R 7	W 2.3
D 4	I 7.3	N 7.5	S 6.5	X 0.3
E 13	J 0.2	O 8	T 9	Y 2
				Z 0.1

which we can now put to a fascinating hybrid effect.

Take a simple example, the 3-letter words. TEE (9 + 13 + 13) totals 35, whereas the Hebrew coin the ZUZ (0.1 + 3.3 + 0.1) is, at a total of 3.5, a tenth of the 'value' of a golf peg.

TEE and ZUZ are the highest and lowest scoring standard 3-letter words and though, for fun, some amazing superlatives will be quoted in due course, this description is centred on everyday words. What, therefore, are the highest and lowest scoring superlatives in other categories of word length up to (say) the 9-letter words?

In standard English, A, I and the poetic exclamation O are the only single-letter words. However, Scotland has the river with the name of E[1] and there are towns in Michigan and in France called Y.

---

[1] Found on Ordnance Survey quarter-inch map number 5 at grid reference NH 5413.

E cannot be outscored but is Y the minimal value word? X-ray, J-pen and Z-bar do not qualify as they are facets of a compound hyphenated word and though each letter may be considered as a self-descriptive name such an argument is less than satisfactory. If you permit obsolete words then Q (see Glossary) will take some beating.

The Scottish word EE is undoubtedly the superlative high-scoring 2-letter word. Intriguingly, the total of 26 for this palindrome is exactly the same as that of two other palindromes, TOT and MADAM. Thus, one need not concern oneself only with contrasts of numerical extremes but with other related curiosities. For example, what is the superlative sumgram (numerical anagram) of TEE? TEE scores 35. What, therefore, is the longest word you can find which also scores 35?

Whilst the wordsmith will pay more attention to the superlatives and add such as EETE (an obsolete spelling of the present tense of the verb EAT) to an ever increasing collection beginning E, EE, TEE, EETE and match these with their ultimate sumgrams, far more fun can be derived from playing with words in general.

Can we find the SEXIEST women in the world? Which women have names which total the same as SEXIEST (55.6)? How about the world's LARGEST (49.8) insects or UGLIEST (44.9) men? Conversely, what adjectives match those whom we admire or cannot tolerate?

What are the relative values of saints and sinners? Which saint and which sinner equate mathematically? Can we discern ideal partners? It is hardly surprising that ROMEO (38.5) and JULIET (37.3) are star-crossed lovers – who would have been a better computer match for either?

One can even play Q-Dye (see page 43) with Sumwords. Begin with a widely contrasting pair such as TEEN (42.5) and QUIZ (11.1) and see if you can take them step by step until you achieve numerical parity.

Those for whom mathematics is more interesting than words can delve into relationships based on Sumwords. For example, FIVE (24.3) is numerically equal to FIFTY (24.3) and SIX (14.1) is the 'smallest' number. Can the numerate hybridizer discover some interesting mathematical paradoxes? ONE (28.5) + TWO (19.3) = 47.8 which is less than THREE (48).

Is it possible to produce a combination of words which make nonsensical mathematics but perfect hybrid sense?

This concept was put to three of the *Countdown* champions who came up with the following:

Michael Wylie

(1) ONE + ? = FOURTEEN (What is ?)   13

(2) SIXTEEN – ? = FOUR (What is that same ?)   12

(3) The 'saintly' CILLA BLACK (46.8) can be equated to two of history's most notorious figures. Who are they?

(4) Beginning with DEER (37) Michael created an ever decreasing in value word ladder which culminated in a word (8.5) which also describes a deer. Only one letter at a time may be changed and, each time, a normal word must result.

(5) A word other than QUIZ which totalled 11.1, another which totalled 22.2, a third which totalled 33.3 and a fourth which totalled 44.4.

Michael's answers are given at the end of the chapter. But, can you match this or even extend it further?

Ivy Dixon-Baird

TEETETET

(1) She provided a 9-letter word which is the sumgram of TEE. Can you equal or better it?

(2) Whilst the SEXIEST woman eluded her, she did find that a famous film star (whose surname includes the letters B and O) could have been such – if only she had taken more care of herself. Who is the very famous thirties star who would certainly be the SEXIEST woman if she had not got B.O.?! Both Christian name and surname are needed.

Darryl Francis

Darryl is the wordsmith's wordsmith. Not for him is the standard family dictionary the ultimate authority. He provided the superlatives for the highest and lowest words in the categories 2-letter to 9-letter and question marks are included where his discoveries happen to be perfectly normal words. To show the range of his study, the dictionaries quoted are those where he found these amazing words.

Highest Scoring

Darryl confirmed EE, TEE and EETE in the 2, 3 and 4 categories to which he added:

5   EETTE (57) *Oxford English Dictionary*
6   TEETEE (70) *Websters New International* (2nd edition)
7   TEETEES (76.5) *Websters New International* (2nd edition)
8   TEETERER (84) *Websters New International* (2nd edition)
9   RESETTERS (84) *Chambers English*

(The ultimate 9-letter word has two hyphens. It scores 96.5. It is standard English and occurs, for example, in the *Concise*. What is it?)

Lowest Scoring

2   ZY (2.1) *Pears Advanced Word-Puzzler's Dictionary*
3   ZZZ (0.3) *Hamlyn Encyclopedic World Dictionary*
4   ZZZZ (0.4) *American Thesaurus of Slang*/OED
5   ? (5.2)
6   ? (15.6)
7   ZYZZYVA (13.8) *The Official Scrabble Players Dictionary*
8   ZIGZAGGY (21.9) *Chambers English*
9   BUZZINGLY (27.6) *Chambers English*

ZYZZYVA is a tropical weevil, but there is a word found in the *Concise* and other standard dictionaries which, by scoring 18.2, runs it a good second in the low scoring 7-letter word category. Can you discover it?

Ignoring ZZZZ (see Glossary), what is the ultimate low scoring conventional 4-letter word? It is an ordinary, everyday word.

By delving into the darker recesses of *Webster Third New International Dictionary* and the *Oxford English Dictionary*, Darryl produced the ultimate Sumwords word ladder. This has the shortest run from the extremes of EETE to ZZZZ:

```
E E T E
F E T E
F I T E
F I T Z
F I Z Z
Z I Z Z
Z Z Z Z
```

If you possess *Chambers English Dictionary* you can make a slightly longer run from EETE to ZZZZ. Choose either chain and, changing one letter at a time to produce an equally valid word, reach the destination of ZZZZ.

EETE	EETE
METE	METE
MOTE	MEZE
?·	?
?	?
?	?
?	?
ZZZZ	ZZZZ

But, it was Darryl's study of sumgrams that displayed his talents to the full. He produced in excess of a hundred groups of sumgrams, all containing words of no fewer than 15 letters each! Just one example will illustrate the amazing skill of this incredible *Countdown* champion. The following six 15-letter words all score exactly the same (101.4):

ACCLIMATISATION, ANTICHRISTIANLY, BIOASTRONAUTICS, DOCTRINARIANISM, FRENCHIFICATION, LOPHOBRANCHIATE

To leave you with a fun challenge, can you find Darryl's pairing of two words? One has seventeen letters, the other has nineteen! They are exact opposites in meaning. Both are standard nouns and either will score 127.9. The 19-letter word can be defined as 'the quality or fact of presenting nothing other than that which is basically simple' – the 17-letter word naturally means the opposite, and both words can be found in the *Concise*.

Finally, if you are attempting Michael Wylie's challenge of discovering words which total 11.1, 22.2, 33.3 etc., then let Darryl provide you with a choice of two words which may well end the chain. Scoring 111.1 are DECONTAMINATION and APPROPRIATENESS.

Peter Newby

ANSWERS

Cryptarithmetic page 120

1. 3 1 3 4
    3 1 3 4
    3 1 3 4 +
    ─────────
    9 4 0 2

2. 2 4 1 5 3
    2 4 1 5 3 +
    ─────────
    4 8 3 0 6

3.   8 2 0
        8 2 0
        8 2 0
        8 2 0 +
        ─────────
        3 2 8 0

Note that 4a can have NEAT as 2104, 2034 or 3241 any of which provide a solution.

4b. 3 2 8 9
     3 2 8 9
     3 2 8 9 +
     ─────────
     9 8 6 7

5. 7 4 8 1 0 2
      9 4 5 5 3 −
    ─────────────
    6 5 3 5 4 9

Sumwords page 123

Michael Wylie

1. NINE
2. NINE
3. ATTILA, HITLER
4. DEER   (37)
    PEER   (36.1)
    PEAR   (31.6)
    BEAR   (30)
    BEAD   (27)
    BEND   (26)
    BAND   (21.5)
    BANK   (18)
    BASK   (17)
    BACK   (14)
    BUCK   (8.5)

5. SUN   (11.1)
    POOP   (22.2)
    JUNIOR   (33.3)
    PUTTER   (44.4)

Ivy Dixon-Baird

1. QUIZZICAL   2. GRETA GAR(BO)

Darryl Francis

1. The ultimate 9-letter word: TETE-A-TETE
2. Lowest scoring 5- and 6-letter words: BUZZY, JUGFUL
3. Another low scoring 7-letter word: ZYMURGY
4. The ultimate low scoring conventional 4-letter word: BUZZ
5. Sumwords word ladder possibilities:

E E T E	or	E E T E
M E T E		M E T E
M O T E		M E Z E
M O Z E		M O Z E
M O Z Z		M O Z Z
M I Z Z		M I Z Z
Z I Z Z		Z I Z Z
Z Z Z Z		Z Z Z Z

6. Sumgrams pairing:
   STRAIGHTFORWARDNESS, EXTRAORDINARINESS

Sum Fun

Before attempting to master the techniques of *Countdown*'s numbers game, it may be more enjoyable to discover some of the truly fascinating amusements which are available to anyone with a rudimentary knowledge of mathematics.

All of the examples given are well within the compass of a bright child, let alone the average adult. Each example is slightly more taxing than the one it follows and the puzzles culminate with three completely new mathematical card games. Even if numbers leave you cold, I can promise you some delightful surprises.

1 MAGIC

Lewis Carroll devised a simple mathematical trick which is impressive beyond belief and the same basis is used by Carol Vorderman for much of her incredible performances with the numbers aspect of *Countdown*.

Choose (say) any five figure number that you wish, write this down and ask someone to keep it concealed. Let us assume that it is 35,981.

Now write down an apparently random four-figure number and ask someone to put underneath it any other four figure number of his or her choice:

	YOU	5984
	1st FRIEND	6251

You now add another number:

YOU	5984
1st FRIEND	6251
YOU	3748

So it continues:

YOU	5984
1st FRIEND	6251
YOU	3748
2nd FRIEND	8362
YOU	1637
3rd FRIEND	5043
YOU	4956
TOTAL	35,981

This, of course, is the concealed number.

How on earth did you do it?

Whatever number you chose, simply remove the first digit and add this to the last digit. 35,981 then becomes 5,984.

As you have removed 30,000 minus 3 from that total so you simply put it back. In other words you need to add 9,999 three times. Re-examine the sum:

$$
\begin{array}{lr}
\text{YOU} & 5984 \\
\text{1st FRIEND} & 6251 \\
\text{YOU} & 3748 \ +
\end{array} \Bigg\} = 9,999
$$

$$
\begin{array}{lr}
\text{2nd FRIEND} & 8362 \\
\text{YOU} & 1637 \ +
\end{array} \Bigg\} = 9,999
$$

$$
\begin{array}{lr}
\text{3rd FRIEND} & 5043 \\
\text{YOU} & 4956 \ +
\end{array} \Bigg\} = 9,999
$$

You can do this with any number.
For example:

$$2,612,804 = 612,806$$
$$+ 999,999 \text{ twice}$$

$$7,489 = 496$$
$$+ 999 \text{ seven times}$$

Try it and you will amaze not only your friends but also yourself!

Carol Vorderman does this on *Countdown*?

If you think about it, it is very logical. Obviously she knows her 75 times table up to 14 (1050) so that if her final target is (say) 444, she automatically selects $6 \times 75 = 450$. Therefore, all she has to do now is subtract 1 from 75 and multiply this by 6 and if both 1 and 6 can be contrived from the remaining figures she has the solution. This is exactly the same mathematical practice as the magic of Lewis Carroll.

If, like me, you appreciate the theory but still fail to achieve the *Countdown* numbers you will love the next piece of mathematical wizardry – the theory has me totally perplexed but I can do the practical side almost blindfolded. If only a Red Indian had coached me for my G.C.E. back in my schooldays . . .

2   AZTEC MULTIPLICATION

The Aztecs were the dominant people of Mexico and the founders of an empire which was at its height when Cortes invaded their lands in 1519. These American Indians of Nahuatian[1] stock considered numbers to be either good or evil, an odd number was good and an even number was evil. As they disliked evil numbers so they eradicated them in their unique and fascinating system of multiplication.

If we consider (say) 4212×89 and do not have a pocket calculator available to provide the answer of 374,868, let us multiply the numbers Aztec fashion. The system is simple. Double the larger number and halve the smaller, ignoring any fractions. Continue to do this until the smaller number reaches one. Then eradicate the 'evil' numbers in the increasing column and simply add together its 'good' numbers.

As it is easier to show the method with a simple sum such as 56×10 (560) let us begin with that before we tackle the more taxing problem of 4212×89:

---

[1] Collectors of trivia may wish to know that the Nahuatl language has provided us with the words AVOCADO, CHILI, CHOCOLATE and TOMATO.

56	10
112	5
224	2
448	1

10 tells us that 56 is evil and 2 tells us that 224 is evil and so these are deleted and the good numbers added together:

~~56~~	10
112	5
~~224~~	2
448	1
——	
560	
——	

Now for the problem of 4212 × 89:

4212	89
~~8424~~	44
~~16848~~	22
33696	11
67392	5
~~134784~~	2
269568	1
——	
374868	
——	

and our pocket calculator agrees!

3   THE MIDDLE AGES

Chambers English Dictionary carries the classic definition for middle-aged. Wittily, it describes the adjective as 'between youth and old age, variously reckoned to suit the reckoner'!

For those of us who might qualify for the description middle-aged, a direct answer to the question of our actual age can be a trifle embarrassing if we believe ourselves to be as young as we think we look. However, an answer of sorts is needed.

Suppose that one is 50. Technically 50 is the last number in a decade beginning with 41 as 1 to 10, 11 to 20, 21 to 30, 31 to 40 etc. constitute decades of ages, so a completely truthful answer is, 'In my forties'. The following year poses a greater problem as 51 cannot be disguised in this fashion. The solution is simple. Multiply 51×5 and divide the result by 7:

Question: 'How old are you?'
Answer: '36,' pause, 'excluding weekends.'

With a cleverly timed pause the subject is changed with good humour and the questioner is none the wiser.

Now reverse the procedure and imagine that you wish to know the age of one who could be described as '39 going on 60'. The following is a neat trick to produce the answer without the other ever being aware of it.

Tell the victim to think of a number between 1 and 9 which you will attempt to discover.

Let us assume that you pose the question in 1990 to a lady born on 1 January 1930 who, of course, is now 60. She chooses the number 7. This she writes down on paper.

Tell her to double it. 14.

Add 5. 19.

Multiply by 50. If she finds this difficult tell her to add a zero and multiply by 5.

Answer 950.

Now she has to add 1,740*. Answer 2690.

Finally, without revealing this to you, she deducts her year of birth:

$$\begin{array}{r} 2690 \\ 1930 - \\ \hline 760 \\ \hline \end{array}$$

You ask her for this answer and immediately tell her that the number she first thought of was 7.

Seven is the first figure in the answer and, though you keep this part to yourself, her age is the last two numbers – 60.

4   THE CLEWLOW FORMULA

Charles Clewlow is an avid fan of *Countdown*. He is well known to the production team as a regular applicant for a ticket to the programme

---

*For 1991 the addition is 1741 and this increases annually.

though few of them are aware of Charles's hobby – he is a codebreaker.

Charles encountered Lewis Carroll's highly complex formula for deducing the day for any given date, and decided to produce another formula simple enough for the mathematically inclined to do in his or her head within a matter of seconds.

The Clewlow Formula of Significant Remainders has one performing some very easy mental arithmetic with the result that the final act of simple division by a 7 gives the day of the week on the basis of:

an exact division = Sunday
a remainder of 1 = Monday
a remainder of 2 = Tuesday
a remainder of 3 = Wednesday
a remainder of 4 = Thursday
a remainder of 5 = Friday
a remainder of 6 = Saturday

All that you require to achieve this is to produce the code number for the year by simple division and relate this to the code number for the month (merely remembering which number applies to which month) and, finally, consider the exact day of the month. Mathematically expressed it is:

$$\frac{\text{YEAR CODE NUMBER + MONTH CODE NUMBER + DAY OF MONTH}}{7}$$

(a) *The code number for the year.* This is given in terms of the twentieth century but adjustments for other centuries will follow.

Ignore the 19 and divide the last two numbers by 4. For example, 1900, 1901, 1902, 1903 cannot be divided by 4 so this first step is ignored.

1904, 1905, 1906, 1907 all produce an answer of 1 with an *insignificant* remainder which is ignored.

1990 is 22 with an *insignificant* remainder.

Add the resultant number to the year, again ignoring the 19. Hence:

1900   00 + 0 =   0
1901   01 + 0 =   1
1990   90 + 22 = 112

Divide this first step year-number by 7 to produce a **significant remainder**:

1900	$0 \div 7 =$	0 with a remainder 0
1901	$1 \div 7 =$	0 with a remainder 1
1990	$112 \div 7 =$	16 with a remainder 0

This **significant remainder** is the code number for the year.

(b) *The code number for the month*. This is the only aspect which you need to commit to memory.

January	0	May	1	September	5
February	3	June	4	October	0
March	3	July	6	November	3
April	6	August	2	December	5

Note: In leap years when calculating a date in January or February 1 has to be subtracted from the final total.

To put the Clewlow Formula into practice let us examine two dates of minor historical significance:

1. **26 October 1917.** Brazil declared war on Germany.

   Year code $1917 = 17$
   $$17 \div 4 = 4 \text{ (ignore remainder)}$$
   $$4 + 17 = 21$$
   $$21 \div 7 = 3 \text{ with a } \textbf{significant remainder}$$
   of 0

   The code number for 1917 is, therefore, 0
   Month code   October is 0
   Day of month 26th
   ∴ *Day of week* $\dfrac{0 + 0 + 26}{7}$

   produces the **significant remainder** of 5 and 5 is a Friday.

   Therefore, Brazil declared war on Germany on a Friday.

2. **18 August 1983.** The world gluttony record for eating a hundred unshelled whelks was achieved in 5 minutes 17 seconds at The Apples and Pears Public House, Liverpool Street Station, London by one John Fletcher.

Year code	$1983 = 83$
	$83 \div 4 = 20$ (ignore remainder)
	$20 + 83 = 103$
	$103 \div 7 = $ a **significant remainder** of 5
Month code	August is 2
Day of month	18th
∴ Day of week	$\dfrac{5 + 2 + 18}{7} = $ a **significant remainder** of 4
	$4 = $ Thursday

A delightful use of the Clewlow Formula is to tell your friends whose 'child' they happen to be on the basis of the traditional rhyme:

> *Monday's child is fair of face,*
> *Tuesday's child is full of grace,*
> *Wednesday's child is full of woe,*
> *Thursday's child has far to go;*
> *Friday's child is loving and giving,*
> *Saturday's child works hard for a living,*
> *But the child that is born on the Sabbath day*
> *Is bonny and blithe and good and gay.*

If your concern is with the nineteenth century, simply add a 2 to the final result and, if the answer is 7 or greater, then divide by 7 again for the **significant remainder**. For the eighteenth century it is rather complicated as 1752 is the shortest year of the Christian Era as far as England and most English-speaking nations are concerned. Calculations from 14 September 1752 inclusive require the addition of 4. The reason concerns the change from the Julian to the Gregorian calendar which resulted in 2 September 1752 being followed by 14 September 1752 and a public outcry at the loss of 11 days and especially the wages for those missing days! Most European Catholic countries had made that change in 1582 whereas Russia still calculated its dates to the system introduced by Julius Caesar in 46 BC (hence the name, Julian) until 1918 and Greece held out against Pope Gregory's reform until 1923. The calculations, therefore, for the historical periods are treated in English terms and a simple table back to the year AD 1000 reads as follows:

1900	– 1999	add 0
1800	– 1899	add 2
1752	– 1799	add 4 (Gregorian)
1700	– 1752	add 1 (Julian)
1600	– 1699	add 2
1500	– 1599	add 3
1400	– 1499	add 4
1300	– 1399	add 5
1200	– 1299	add 6
1100	– 1199	add 0
1000	– 1099	add 1

Thereafter, add in the sequence of simple additions of one number to 6, then 0, then 1 to 6. As the Julian calendar had leap years in such as 1700 in England (but not Scotland[1] or Catholic Europe) so the minus 1 factor applies to January and February in all of the years ending with a double zero. Julian leap years were first included in AD 4 so this table can be extended quite easily to the year AD 1.

Thus, to put the historical dates to the test, we should find that whatever the 2 September 1752 happens to be then the 14 September 1752 will be the following day. Our formula, therefore, is:

$$\left(\frac{\text{YEAR CODE} + \text{MONTH CODE} + \text{DAY}}{7}\right) + \text{CENTURY CODE}$$

2 September 1752

Year code	1752	= 52
	52 ÷ 4	= 13
	13 + 52	= 65
	65 ÷ 7	= 9 with a **significant remainder** of 2
Month code	September is 5	
Day of month	2nd	
∴ *Day of week*	$\dfrac{2 + 5 + 2}{7}$	= a **significant remainder** of 2

Now add the century code of 1 (Julian calendar)
This equals 3.   3 = Wednesday

---

[1]Scotland, apart from St. Kilda, made the change in 1600 which resulted in the loss of ten days. The British colonies, including North America, made the change at the same time as England. St. Kilda made the change in 1912 which meant the loss of 13 days.

14 September 1752

Year code	Exactly the same as above = 2
Month code	Exactly the same as above = 5
Day of month	14th
∴ *Day of week*	$\dfrac{2 + 5 + 14}{7}$ = a **significant remainder** of 0

Now add the century code of 4 (Gregorian calendar)
This equals 4.   4 = Thursday.

This could be a mere unprovable coincidence so let us try again, this time where we know the day for certain. Pepys recorded in his famous *Diary* that the Great Fire of London began on the 'Lord's Day', 2 September 1666. Therefore, our final result should give us 'zero' for Sunday.

Year code	1666 = 66
	16 ÷ 4 = 16 (ignore remainder)
	16 + 66 = 82
	82 ÷ 7 = 11 with a **significant remainder** of 5
Month code	September is 5
Day of month	2nd
∴ *Day of week*	$\dfrac{5 + 5 + 2}{7}$ = a **significant remainder** of 5

Now add the century code of 2.   2 + 5 = 7
The day code goes from 'an exact division' up to a 'remainder of 6'. 7 is an 'exact division' of 7, so it has to be Sunday.

For the twenty-first century subtract 1 or add 6. Charles says that you get the same result either way!

5   MAGIC SQUARES

Many readers will have come across the classic puzzle which requires the placing within a 3 × 3 grid of the numerals 1 to 9 so that the total of 15 can be read in any direction – horizontal, vertical or diagonal. One solution is as follows:

8	1	6
3	5	7
4	9	2

Now try some Newby specials, all devised by a writer who failed his maths O level three times so they cannot be that difficult.

(a)

Using only the numerals 1 to 9 to which are added fractions totalling 1½ create a Magic Square in which the total of each and every line is 15½.

(b)

Choosing any nine numbers from 1 to 10 create a Magic Square which totals 16 in any direction.

(c)

Choosing any nine numbers from 1 to 14 create a Magic Square which totals 30 in any direction.

(d)

Choosing any nine numbers from 1 to 20 create a Magic Square which totals 48 in any direction.

(e)

Without using a three figure number create a Magic Square which totals 285 in every possible direction.

(f)

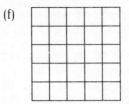

Using the numbers 1 to 25 create a Magic Square which totals 65 in every possible direction.

The solutions to the above are given at the end of this chapter.

6   THE ROUND OF DRINKS

John Meade entertained Carol Vorderman and Sylvia Syms to a great evening in a bar near the Yorkshire Television studios. He is a generous fellow but, on sighting the bill for £30, he remembered that, being a true television producer, he had to be mindful of his budget and decreed that each must pay his or her share.

In consequence, Newby (who was moonlighting as a waiter) took £10 from each of them and was just about to put this money in the till when the bar manager told him that he had overcharged by £5.

A resourceful fellow, Newby decided to slip £2 into his pocket, ring £25 into the till and return £3 to the drinkers at the table. So he gave John a pound, Carol a pound and Sylvia a pound. This meant that John had now paid £9, Carol £9 and Sylvia £9. Three nines are 27, plus £2 in the waiter's pocket makes £29. Whatever happened to that remaining pound?

An explanation is given on page 144 together with a written apology to three charming friends who insist that this is a tissue of lies – John would not have paid a penny!

7   MATHEMATICAL TRICKS

One or more players can enjoy training themselves for the numbers aspect of *Countdown* with a pack of cards containing at least one joker.

Three different games are described, each is completely original and appearing in print for the first time. In essence, these are numerate solitaire, rummy and poker all based on the same values for the cards:

> The joker represents   100
> The king represents   75
> The queen represents   50
> The jack represents   25
> All others as face value.

(a) Yorkshire Patience

This is pure *Countdown* training for the serious aspirant to the programme.

Separate the pack into two decks, one containing the court cards and the joker(s) with all of the other cards including the aces (which represent one) in a second deck. The decks are shuffled and placed face down on the table. Paper and pencil may be used if desired.

Give yourself a fixed target figure (say) 456. Deal yourself five standard cards and one court card. Now attempt to score 456 using any combination of any of these cards. Suppose that you have an ace, a three, a seven, two eights and a queen (50).

$$\text{first } 8 \times \text{queen} = 400$$
$$\text{second } 8 \times \text{seven} = 56 +$$
$$\overline{456}$$

You have won a trick. This is placed on one side to your credit. Your hand now contains an ace and a three. Replenish from the decks and continue the process.

However, suppose that you are now unable to create 456 with the cards to hand. You jettison the complete set which becomes a negative trick. Negative tricks cancel positive tricks and the object of your task is to see if you can run through the joint decks and finish with a positive result.

You may, if you wish, award yourself imperfect tricks which total within ten either side of your target figure. Thus, any total between 446 to 466 is acceptable for 456.

(b) Yorkshire Rummy

This time you do not separate the cards. A target figure is agreed and six cards are dealt to each player. The remaining cards are placed face down on the table and the top card exposed.

Ideally, four numerate quick thinkers are in competition as one tardy player can destroy the fun. Appreciate that the fourth to play has the greatest thinking time, so that whoever is in charge of the action at any one time does, by making a play, create thinking time for himself or herself. Thus, a player without (say) a court card should make an immediate change of card from his or her hand for either the exposed card or the unknown one at the top of the deck.

Players may lay perfect tricks at any time but may only replenish their hands when it is their particular turn. If you, for example, create a perfect trick from four cards then you collect four fresh cards when it is your turn to play. This means that players either replenish cards or else make single card changes.

At the end of the game, the winner must prove the validity of his or her tricks.

(c) Yorkshire Poker
Both perfect and imperfect tricks are in contention.

A target figure is agreed. Six cards are dealt to each player. Players now gamble with tokens or even with money. All who wish to participate pay into the kitty.

The participants may now be dealt as many or as few replacement cards as they wish. Gambling continues until only two players remain.

When one of the two remaining players pays to see the other's hand, that player must now state the figure that he or she has in mind and prove it to the satisfaction of the table. An error in maths forfeits the round and the last remaining player does *not* need to expose his or her cards in order to collect the kitty. Assuming, however, that both players are mathematically accurate then the winner is the one closer to the target figure. In the event of a tie, both players make simple totals of their hands and the one nearer to the target is the winner.

There is no arbitrary limit to imperfection of a trick.

Peter Newby

ANSWERS

Magic Squares page 139

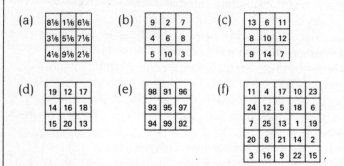

(a)

8⅙	1⅙	6⅙
3⅙	5⅙	7⅙
4⅙	9⅙	2⅙

(b)

9	2	7
4	6	8
5	10	3

(c)

13	6	11
8	10	12
9	14	7

(d)

19	12	17
14	16	18
15	20	13

(e)

98	91	96
93	95	97
94	99	92

(f)

11	4	17	10	23
24	12	5	18	6
7	25	13	1	19
20	8	21	14	2
3	16	9	22	15

The Round of Drinks page 141

The short answer is that the pound is in the till.

The trick lies in the phrasing. Instead of stating, 'Three nines are twenty-seven *plus* two pounds...', the correct form is 'Three nines are twenty-seven *minus* two pounds...' which brings the sum to £25. £25 + £2 + £3 = £30.

This classic puzzle would have had, in the days when it was originally posed, each drinker paying £8 6s. 8d. if the correct price had been quoted from the outset. With today's metric pound the division is £8.33⅓ and what really baffles me is which of the three drinkers would have paid a penny more than the others in order to cope with the division of a new penny into thirds? Meanwhile, humble apologies to the victims and, doubtless, John will have the last word after Carol and Sylvia have made their comments to him on the standards of service they encounter in Yorkshire.

Classic Countdown *Games*

As you have learned, over the years *Countdown* has produced some brilliant exponents of the game. Some, like Michael Wylie, impressed more with their numerical skills. Mark Nyman, as I mentioned earlier, with his expertise in spotting the Conundrum as soon as the letters are revealed. Allan Saldanha and Tim Morrissey for their youthful mastery. When players of this calibre have been pitched together the games have not been necessarily high scoring; their skills have often cancelled each other out, but, my, have they come up with some classics!

In selecting my choice of 'Classic *Countdown* Games', out of nearly a thousand, I have taken many factors into consideration. The selection of letters and, of course, the degree of difficulty regarding the random numbers game and the Conundrum is of paramount importance. Who was playing who? What risks, if any, were taken?

So enjoy and marvel over the next few pages, the skills of the greatest Countdowners.

COUNTDOWN FINAL – Series 6
Olivia Lloyd-Potts versus Darryl Francis

This game is remarkable in that neither Conundrum was solved and yet Darryl still managed a fair total of 69 points for his victory. Even so, 69 points could have been bettered. For example, in round five, both players offered 5-letter words yet GAMBOGE would have given either of them 7 points. I have highlighted two further rounds (one involving words, the other is a numbers game) and provided improved results at the end of this chapter. To compete, cover the right-hand side of the page. Can you beat the champions?

Challenge Faced	Olivia		Darryl	

1 | S | D | T | P | A | E | E | B | I |

PASTED 0 DEBATES 7

2 | L | S | H | A | E | A | B | G | I |

SLEIGH 6 / 6 GABLES 6 / 13

3 | 7 | 2 | 8 | 1 | 9 | 75 | | 559 |

555 0 / 6 560 7 / 20

(Darryl: $8 - 2 = 6 - 1 = 5 + 75 = 80 \times 7 = 560$)

4 | O | E | O | S | P | T | V | J | S |

STOVES 6 / 12 STOOPS 6 / 26

5 | B | G | N | G | A | E | O | X | M |

BEGAN 5 / 17 AMONG 5 / 31

6 | 4 | 8 | 1 | 9 | 100 | 50 | | 537 |

541 0 / 17 540 7 / 38

(Darryl: $4 + 1 = 5$ $100 + 8 = 108 \times 5 = 540$)
It is possible to produce 537. *See page* 166

7 | A | A | A | T | R | C | N | L | H |

failed 0 / 17 *failed* 0 / 38

(The Conundrum was CHARLATAN)

8 | Q | V | N | R | E | A | I | S | L |

RAVINES 0 / 17 RAVELINS 8 / 46

9 | U | I | A | U | R | Y | C | M | O |

CURIO 5 / 22 AURIC 5 / 51

10 | 9 | 4 | 5 | 7 | 75 | 100 | | 321 |

321 10
———
32

322 0
———
51

(Olivia: $4 \times 100 = 400 - 75 = 325 - (9 - 5) = 321$)

11 | C | V | T | F | E | O | A | T | I |

EVICT 5
———
37

COVET 5
———
56

Higher scoring words given on page 166

12 | E | U | E | G | D | G | M | S | B |

BESMUDGE 0
invalid ———
37

BUDGES 6
———
62

13 | 2 | 10 | 10 | 4 | 3 | 50 | | 801 |

796 0
———
37

800 7
———
69

(Darryl: $2 \times 4 = 8 \times 10 \times 10 = 800$)
(Carol Vorderman: $10 + 10 = 20 - 4 = 16 \times 50 = 800$
$3 - 2 = 1 \quad 800 + 1 = 801$)

14 | S | H | O | U | T | C | O | A | L |

failed 0
———
37

failed 0
———
69

(The Conundrum was HOLOCAUST)

COUNTDOWN FINAL – Series 7
Ian Bebbington versus Julian Hough

A classically entertaining final. With three rounds to go Julian was trailing by 30 points. To win he had to obtain 18 points for a 9-letter word in the final letters round, then score points in the numbers game without Ian scoring, and, finally, get the Conundrum. He failed only at the last hurdle.

The highlighted rounds are numbers 10 and 13.

Challenge Faced	**Ian**	**Julian**

1 | P | T | S | T | L | I | E | N | U |

SPITTLE 7   SPITTLE 7

2 | Y | T | B | E | A | T | O | A | G | BATTY $\dfrac{5}{12}$ BEGOT $\dfrac{5}{12}$

3 | 4 | 1 | 2 | 6 | 25 | 50 | | 317 | 317 $\dfrac{10}{22}$ 317 $\dfrac{10}{22}$

$(6 \times 50 = 300 + 25 = 325 \quad 4 \times 2 = 8 \quad 325 - 8 = 317)$

4 | H | B | F | R | E | E | I | E | A | BEEFIER $\dfrac{7}{29}$ HEIFER $\dfrac{0}{22}$

5 | I | T | L | T | E | N | G | A | P | PLEATING $\dfrac{8}{37}$ PLEATING $\dfrac{8}{30}$

6 | 9 | 10 | 1 | 4 | 5 | 25 | | 374 | 374 $\dfrac{10}{47}$ 374 $\dfrac{10}{40}$

$(10 + 5 = 15 \times 25 = 375 - 1 = 374)$

7 | M | M | U | L | E | D | F | O | X | FLUMMOXED $\dfrac{10}{57}$ *failed* $\dfrac{0}{40}$

8 | W | S | M | U | S | I | E | Q | A | MISUSE $\dfrac{6}{63}$ SWIMS $\dfrac{0}{40}$

9 | D | B | S | Y | I | O | A | W | I | DAISY $\dfrac{5}{68}$ BAWDY $\dfrac{5}{45}$

10 | 6 | 4 | 9 | 7 | 8 | 25 | | 690 | 691 $\dfrac{7}{75}$ 691 $\dfrac{7}{52}$

$176 \times 4 = 700$

$(7 \times 4 = 28 \times 25 = 700 - 9 = 691)$
It is possible to produce 690. See page 166

11 | N | B | G | N | F | L | O | A | I | LOAFING $\dfrac{7}{82}$ BALING $\dfrac{0}{52}$

12 | C | N | T | Y | T | E | I | A | R | CATTERY   0   CERTAINTY   18
                                                    —   —
                                                    82   70

13 | 5 | 10 | 7 | 6 | 50 | 25 | | 923 | 925   0   924   7
                                                    —   —
                                                    82   77

(Julian: $25 - 5 = 20 \times 50 = 1000$ $10 \times 7 = 70 + 6 = 76$
$1000 - 76 = 924$)

It is possible to produce 923. See page 166

14 | T | E | E | U | P | L | A | T | E | *failed*   0   *failed*   0
                                                        —   —
                                                        82   77

(The Conundrum was EPAULETTE)

COUNTDOWN FINAL – Series 8
Clive Spate versus Anthony Butcher

A one-sided final but few could have lived with Clive Spate in this form. He amassed 107 points but, incredibly, he missed the chance of additional points even allowing for his disallowed word in round 4.

In one of the rounds there was a 9-letter word available and in at least two of the other rounds there were opportunities for either player to improve upon the words he submitted. These are highlighted. As I mentioned previously, nouns formed from verbs by the addition of the suffix -ER are a problem and Clive was very lucky in having his round 9 submission accepted. Played with the same edition of the dictionary today, his word would have been rejected. If you are competing, therefore, you may assume that he scored 'nil' for that round.

Challenge Faced   **Clive**   **Anthony**

1 | O | A | E | L | G | D | S | I | N | DEALINGS   8   DEALINGS   8

For the highest-scoring word see page 166

2 | S | C | R | A | T | U | S | N | X |

CARTS 5

13

CARTS 5

13

Higher-scoring words are given on page 166

3 | 7 | 7 | 10 | 4 | 75 | 50 | | 365 |

367 0

13

365 10

23

(Anthony: $50 + 75 = 125$ $7 - 4 = 3 \times 125 = 375 - 10 = 365$)

4 | E | A | O | R | H | L | T | E | S |

EARHOLES 0
invalid

13

LEATHERS 8

31

5 | P | D | S | A | W | I | S | P | E |

SWAPPED 7

20

SWAPPED 7

38

6 | 1 | 4 | 10 | 3 | 50 | 100 | | 475 |

475 10

30

declared 0
nothing

38

(Clive: $100 + 50 + 10 = 160$ $160 \times 3 = 480$ $480 - 4 = 476$
$476 - 1 = 475$)

7 | T | R | A | G | I | C | I | E | R |

GERIATRIC 10

40

failed 0

38

8 | S | T | N | A | T | E | Y | W | I |

SATINET 7

47

TWINES 0

38

9 | O | I | E | D | M | T | N | A | R |

DOMINATER 18

65

DOMINATE 0

38

10 | 8 | 5 | 7 | 3 | 75 | 25 | | 698 |

698 10

75

698 10

48

($25 + 75 = 100 \times 7 = 700$ $5 - 3 = 2$ $700 - 2 = 698$)

11 | B D E N V R O V A | BROADEN 7 | BRAVED 0

$$\frac{}{82} \qquad \frac{}{48}$$

12 | O U L G V E O M W | GLOVE 5 | GLOVE 5

$$\frac{}{87} \qquad \frac{}{53}$$

A higher-scoring word is given on page 166

13 | 8 10 3 4 100 50 | 548 | 548 10 | 546 0

$$\frac{}{97} \qquad \frac{}{53}$$

(Clive: 50 + 4 = 54 × 10 = 540 + 8 = 548)

14 | A L B U M H I N T | THUMBNAIL 10 | *failed* 0

$$\frac{}{107} \qquad \frac{}{53}$$

COUNTDOWN FINAL – Series 9
Mick Keeble versus David Trace

A marvellous example of fighting spirit by David Trace. Going into the first Conundrum he was 35 points down. He solved it to gain 10 points and then it was Mick Keeble's turn to flag as David, bit by bit, pulled back until, going into the final Conundrum, he trailed Mick by just 4 points, 74–70. David won. Both a numbers and a word round are highlighted.

Challenge Faced | **Mick** | **David**

1 | Y C I L H F A N T | FAINTLY 7 | FAINTLY 7

2 | S D O I R T E T A | TOASTER 7 | DISTORT 7

$$\frac{}{14} \qquad \frac{}{14}$$

Higher-scoring words are given on page 166

3 | 8 5 10 3 25 75 | 710 | 710 10 | *declared* 0
| | | | *nothing*

$$\frac{}{24} \qquad \frac{}{14}$$

(Mick: 75 × 10 = 750 8 × 5 = 40 750 − 40 = 710)

4 | N | A | L | H | O | M | Y | E | S | MANHOLES $\frac{8}{32}$ HOMELY $\frac{0}{14}$

5 | R | N | T | A | E | K | P | U | T | PATTERN $\frac{7}{39}$ TANKER $\frac{0}{14}$

6 | 6 | 1 | 9 | 7 | 2 | 75 | | 214 | 214 $\frac{10}{49}$ 212 $\frac{0}{14}$

(Mick: $75 \times 2 = 150$ $9 \times 7 = 63 + 1 = 64 + 150 = 214$)

7 | M | O | R | E | S | H | A | P | E | *failed* $\frac{0}{49}$ SEMAPHORE $\frac{10}{24}$

8 | S | C | R | E | I | G | V | A | L | GRAVES $\frac{0}{49}$ CLAVIERS $\frac{8}{32}$

9 | T | U | G | W | P | O | A | T | L | GLOAT $\frac{0}{49}$ OUTLAW $\frac{6}{38}$

10 | 2 | 6 | 1 | 7 | 8 | 50 | | 105 | 105 $\frac{10}{59}$ 105 $\frac{10}{48}$

($2 \times 50 = 100$ $6 - 1 = 5 + 100 = 105$)

11 | R | N | B | E | A | S | G | I | R | BEARINGS $\frac{8}{67}$ BEARINGS $\frac{8}{56}$

12 | D | U | C | A | N | R | O | P | I | CANDOUR $\frac{7}{74}$ CANDOUR $\frac{7}{63}$

13 | 8 | 5 | 5 | 4 | 75 | 100 | | 664 | 662 $\frac{0}{74}$ 663 $\frac{7}{70}$

(David: $5 + 4 = 9 \times 75 = 675$ $100 \div 5 = 20 - 8 = 12$
$675 - 12 = 663$)

It is *possible to produce* 664. *See page* 166

14 | C A B A N A R C H | *failed* 0   CHARABANC 10
                                  74   80

COUNTDOWN FINAL – Series 11
David Reid versus John Clarke

A solid workmanlike performance from John Clarke took him to victory even though he missed out on a Conundrum and a numbers game. Gambling on problematic prefixes available for words in two of the games gave him the edge. Only one words and one numbers round have been highlighted but, for example, that good old *Countdown* standby, DARIOLES, is hidden away elsewhere.

Challenge Faced	David	John
1	S O T I L E W A F	FLOATS 6	FLOATS 6
2	N V T U E A G N O	TONNAGE 7 / 13	TONNAGE 7 / 13
3	9 3 5 4 1 100 **464**	464 10 / 23	464 10 / 23

$(9 + 3 = 12 \quad 5 - 1 = 4 + 12 = 16 + 100 = 116 \times 4 = 464)$

4	T I S A N E X U S	STAINS 0 / 23	UNSEATS 7 / 30
5	P M R A I E G R A	MIRAGE 0 / 23	MARRIAGE 8 / 38
6	5 4 9 2 10 100 **137**	137 10 / 33	137 10 / 48

$(9 \times 5 = 45 + 100 = 145 \quad 10 - 2 = 8 \quad 145 - 8 = 137)$

7 **H E A D I N G U S**   *failed* 0   *failed* 0

$$\overline{33} \qquad \overline{48}$$

(The Conundrum was ANGUISHED)

8 **D S S A E I T L N**   STAINED 7   DETAILS 7

$$\overline{40} \qquad \overline{55}$$

Higher-scoring words are given on page 166

9 **R D L R T O E I U**   TORRID 0   OUTRIDER 8

$$\overline{40} \qquad \overline{63}$$

10 **5 4 6 2 1 25**   **946**   950 7   *declared* 0   *nothing* 63

$$\overline{49}$$

(David: $6 + 4 = 10$ $5 - 1 = 4 \times 10 = 40 - 2 = 38 \times 25 = 950$)

It is possible to produce 946. See page 166

11 **B N F O A I C N E**   FINANCE 7   FINANCE 7

$$\overline{56} \qquad \overline{70}$$

12 **Z A R O S I L D E**   SOLDIER 7   SOLDIER 7

$$\overline{63} \qquad \overline{77}$$

13 **7 6 7 8 3 75**   **315**   314 0   315 10

$$\overline{63} \qquad \overline{87}$$

($7 - 3 = 4 \times 75 = 300$ $7 + 8 = 15 + 300 = 315$)

14 **L O C A L T I E S**   *failed* 0   OSCILLATE 10

$$\overline{63} \qquad \overline{97}$$

COUNTDOWN FINAL – Series 13
Kevin Nelson versus Hilary Hopper

Another close match fought between two unfancied players.

Hilary got off to a bad start when her very first word was disallowed because she had seen a letter which was not there. Then it was nip and tuck until round 10 where she gained the lead. It all depended on the final Conundrum. Hilary pressed the buzzer. I have highlighted five of the rounds.

Challenge Faced	Kevin		Hilary	
1 `T R I O U I N F X`	FRONT	5	RATION	0

erroneous
A *higher-scoring word is given on page* 166

| 2 `G E T I D E B T G` | BEGGED | 6 | BETIDE | 6 |
| | | 11 | | 6 |

| 3 `6 9 3 2 5 75` `474` | 474 | 10 | 474 | 10 |
| | | 21 | | 16 |

$(9 - 5 = 4 + 75 = 79 \times 6 = 474)$

| 4 `F L H A E O P N A` | PANEL | 5 | PANEL | 5 |
| | | 26 | | 21 |

Higher-scoring words are given on page 166

| 5 `V I T E N I S A Y` | VANITIES | 8 | VANITIES | 8 |
| | | 34 | | 29 |

| 6 `4 5 8 9 6 50` `766` | 765 | 7 | 765 | 7 |
| | | 41 | | 36 |

$(9 + 6 = 15 \quad 5 - 4 = 1 + 50 = 51 \times 15 = 765)$
It is possible to produce 766. *See page* 166

7 | T A M I L R O A D | *failed* 0   *failed* 0

                             41   36

(The Conundrum was MALADROIT)

8 | B E S A D E V N D | DEBASED 7   DEBASED 7

                             48   43

9 | R I M A P E H S A | HARPIES 7   HAMPERS 7

                             55   50

Higher-scoring words are given on page 166

10 | 6 4 10 3 8 75 | | 234 | 235 0   234 10

                             55   60

(Hilary: $8 \div 4 = 2$ $6 - 2 = 3 + 75 = 78 \times 3 = 234$)

11 | R I W A B E R T N | TRAINER 7   TAWNIER 7

                             62   67

A *higher-scoring word is given on page 166*

12 | K C W N O I U G D | DUCKING 7   DUCKING 7

                             69   74

13 | 5 4 7 8 6 50 | | 485 | 485 10   485 10

                             79   84

($6 + 4 = 10 \times 50 = 500$ $7 + 8 = 15$ $500 - 15 = 485$)

14 | B L I N D B R I G | *failed* 0   DRIBBLING 10

                             79   94

COUNTDOWN FINAL – Series 16
Roger Wales versus Tony Vick

I include this game as Tony Vick, who had quietly made his way to the final, played an almost perfect all-round game. He solved both Conundrums and missed out on just one numbers game. Three rounds have been highlighted.

Challenge Faced	Roger		Tony	
1 `S T N A E A G L R`	STRANGE	0	STRANGLE	8
2 `T D N S E U L D A`	SALUTED	0	UNSADDLE	8
		0		16
3 `4 5 6 9 3 75` `300`	300	10	300	10
		10		26

$$(4 \times 75 = 300)$$

4 `V H N O I T A V E`	HAVEN	5	HAVEN	5
		15		31

Higher-scoring words are given on page 167

5 `S T W L O R I Q E`	LOITERS	7	TROWELS	7
		22		38
6 `4 9 1 7 1 50` `556`	557	7	557	7
		29		45

$$(9 + 1 = 10 \quad 50 + 4 + 1 = 55 \times 10 = 550 + 7 = 557)$$
It is possible to produce 556. *See page* 167

7 `O N A S C R E E N`	*failed*	0	RESONANCE	10
		29		55

8 | P | S | C | A | D | I | S | O | R | SPORADIC   8   SPORADIC   8
                                                        —   —
                                                        37   63

9 | Z | G | F | A | E | E | N | F | I | AGIN   0   GAFFE   5
                                                     —   —
                                                     37   68

Higher-scoring words are given on page 167

10 | 3 | 1 | 2 | 10 | 7 | 100 | | 529 | 529   10   529   10
                                                   —   —
                                                   47   78

$(100 \div 2 = 50 + 3 = 53 \times 10 = 530 - 1 = 529)$

11 | P | L | G | B | I | E | S | I | L | GILLIES   7   BILLIES   7
                                                      —   —
                                                      54   85

12 | J | D | A | Y | H | A | E | B | O | HEADY   5   BEADY   5
                                                    —   —
                                                    59   90

13 | 3 | 9 | 8 | 1 | 9 | 100 | | 544 | 544   10   540   0
                                                  —   —
                                                  69   90

(Roger: $8 - 3 = 5$ $100 + 9 = 109 \times 5 = 545 - 1 = 544$)

14 | T | E | D | S | T | R | Y | I | N | *failed*   0   DENTISTRY   10
                                                       —   —
                                                       69   100

CHAMPIONSHIP OF CHAMPIONS FINAL – (Held in Series 5)
Mark Nyman versus Joyce Cansfield

When these two contestants fought their way to the first ever
Championship of Champions final, we thought that we would be in
for a very close game. Mark Nyman, beaten only once in 13 games;
Joyce Cansfield, the first ever *Countdown* Champion. Both top
Scrabble players. But, it was not to be that close. Mark played a
flawless game. Only one numbers round has been highlighted.

Challenge Faced		Mark		Joyce	
1	G E M I L A O R F	FOLIAGE	7	FORMAL	0
2	T A D U W S E P D	WASTED	6	WASTED	6
			13		6
3	I G O S E G Y E T	EGGIEST	7	EGGIEST	7
			20		13
4	8 2 7 3 10 75 646	648	7	*declared*	0
			27	*nothing*	13

(Mark: $3 \times 2 = 6$ $6 + 75 = 81$ $81 \times 8 = 648$)

It is possible to produce 646. See page 167

5	U B S I L F A B S	FIBULAS	7	BULBS	0
			34		13
6	D E B O L A W L U	ALLOWED	7	ALLOWED	7
			41		20
7	I P A F C U G X E	FACE	4	FACE	4
			45		24
8	3 1 7 1 5 4 75 693	693	10	693	10
			55		34

($3 - 1 = 2$ $2 + 75 = 77$ $4 + 5 = 9$ $9 \times 77 = 693$)

9	B A L R O O U I S	LABORIOUS	10	*failed*	0
			65		34

(Note that, unlike the preceding series finals and the following Championship of Champions finals, this was a half-hour programme with fewer rounds.)

CHAMPIONSHIP OF CHAMPIONS FINALS – (Held in Series 9)
Clive Freedman versus Peter Evans

Probably the most light-hearted final ever was played between these two genial but brilliant Countdowners.

Going into the final Conundrum Clive needed 10 points to tie. He succeeded then won the tie-breaker to win the championship. Only one words round is highlighted but three of the numbers games needed Carol Vorderman to provide perfect solutions.

	Challenge Faced	Clive		Peter	
1	R D S R I C A E L	CRADLERS *invalid*	0	LARDERS	7
2	T W F U A N D E H	UNTHAWED *invalid*	0 / 0	HAUNTED	7 / 14
3	5 8 3 8 6 25 · 539	542	7 / 7	*declared nothing*	0 / 14

(Clive: $8 + 8 = 16$ $16 + 6 = 22$ $22 \times 25 = 550$ $5 + 3 = 8$
$550 - 8 = 542$)

It is possible to produce 539. See page 167

	Challenge Faced	Clive		Peter	
4	G E E Y D M T I S	MIDGETS	7 / 14	STYMIED	7 / 21
5	G N V A E A S R O	RAVAGES	7 / 21	ORANGES	7 / 28
6	5 8 9 6 4 25 · 244	244	10 / 31	244	10 / 38

$(6 + 4 = 10$ $10 \times 25 = 250$ $9 + 5 = 14$ $14 - 8 = 6$ $250 - 6 = 244)$

	Challenge Faced	Clive		Peter	
7	A M O D E L A R M	*failed*	0 / 31	MELODRAMA	10 / 48

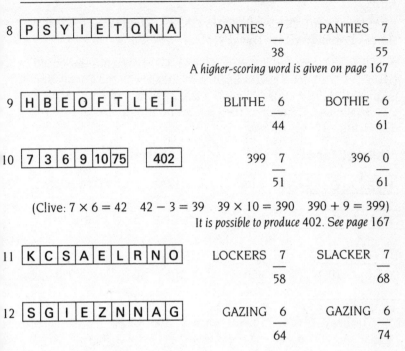

8 P S Y I E T Q N A   PANTIES 7   PANTIES 7

38   55

A higher-scoring word is given on page 167

9 H B E O F T L E I   BLITHE 6   BOTHIE 6

44   61

10 7 3 6 9 10 75   402   399 7   396 0

51   61

(Clive: $7 \times 6 = 42$ $42 - 3 = 39$ $39 \times 10 = 390$ $390 + 9 = 399$)

It is possible to produce 402. *See page* 167

11 K C S A E L R N O   LOCKERS 7   SLACKER 7

58   68

12 S G I E Z N N A G   GAZING 6   GAZING 6

64   74

13 4 4 5 5 9 50   837   840 7   840 7

71   81

(Clive: $4 \times 4 = 16 \times 50 = 800$ $9 \times 5 = 45 - 5 = 40$

$800 + 40 = 840$)

(Peter: $9 + 4 + 4 = 17 \times 50 = 850 - 5 = 845 - 5 = 840$)

It is possible to produce 837. *See page* 167

14 A P E X J O U S T   JUXTAPOSE 10   *failed* 0

81   81

As both contestants had a score of 81 points another Conundrum was played.

15 A N G L E H O A X   HEXAGONAL 10   *failed* 0

91   81

CHAMPIONSHIP OF CHAMPIONS FINAL – (Held in Series 13)
Harvey Freeman versus David Trace

Probably the most exciting game that *Countdown* has produced. David took a 10-point lead going into the break with the Conundrum. In game 9 Harvey pulled 8 points back when David's 'ERRATICLY' was disallowed. Going into the final round it all depended on the Conundrum. Harvey triumphed.

Challenge Faced	Harvey		David	
1 H S T O E A D I N	HEDONIST	8	HANDIEST	8
2 P N H O E N K I M	PHONE	5	PHONE	5
		13		13
3 9 4 4 10 10 25 950	950	10	950	10
		23		23

(Harvey: 25 × 4 = 100   9 − 4 = 5   100 − 5 = 95 × 10 = 950)
(David: 4 + 4 = 8   10 − 8 = 2   10 + 9 = 19 × 2 = 38 × 25 = 950)

4 R T D I A O N E R	RATIONED	8	RATIONED	8
		31		31
5 L S T A E I R F S	REALISTS	8	REALISTS	8
		39		39
6 2 5 3 2 8 75 989	987	7	987	7
		46		46

(8 + 5 = 13 × 75 = 975   2 × 2 = 4 × 3 = 12 + 975 = 987)

7 A E R I A L G U N	*failed*	0	NEURALGIA	10
		46		56
8 R D S O I G U N H	SHROUDING	18	SHROUDING	18
		64		74

9 | C | R | Y | I | E | A | R | T | L | LITERACY 8   ERRATICLY 0
                                                  —   *invalid* —
                                                  72   74

10 | 6 | 4 | 5 | 8 | 3 | 100 | | 425 | 425 10   425 10
                                                —   —
                                                82   84

$(100 - 8 = 92 - 4 = 88 - 3 = 85 \times 5 = 425)$

11 | D | G | M | E | I | S | A | G | E | MIDGES 6   DEMISE 6
                                               —   —
                                               88   90

12 | R | C | G | A | I | U | V | O | E | COURAGE 7   COURAGE 7
                                               —   —
                                               95   97

13 | 7 | 5 | 2 | 8 | 1 | 100 | | 219 | 219 10   219 10
                                               —   —
                                               105   107

$(100 + 7 = 107 \times 2 = 214 + 5 = 219)$

14 | P | U | R | S | U | E | P | A | T | SUPPURATE 10   *failed* 0
                                                —   —
                                                115   107

One last classic encounter. The format differs as it is a breakfast programme with three rounds on a Monday, followed by three rounds on a Tuesday and so on throughout the week culminating in the final three rounds on a Friday.

COUNTDOWN MASTERS – from Series 1 of Channel 4 Daily
Tim Morrissey versus Allan Saldanha

This was the game all *Countdown aficionados* wanted to see. The battle of the young giants. Allan, at ten, the beaten finalist in Series 15 and 12-year-old Tim Morrissey, a semi-finalist in Series 17. We were not to be disappointed. Only one numbers round is highlighted.

Challenge Faced	Tim		Allan	

1 | L | G | S | Q | I | E | E | T | A |

LEGATES 7 — LEGATES 7

2 | 8 | 10 | 6 | 10 | 8 | 5 | | 342 |

Tim: 342 $\frac{10}{17}$

Allan: 342 $\frac{10}{17}$

$(8 \times 5 = 40 - 6 = 34 \times 10 = 340 \quad 10 - 8 = 2 + 340 = 342)$

3 | B | A | B | E | L | D | A | T | E |

Tim: *failed* $\frac{0}{17}$ Allan: DEBATABLE $\frac{10}{27}$

4 | P | S | G | A | U | I | M | N | S |

Tim: ASSUMING $\frac{8}{25}$ Allan: ASSUMING $\frac{8}{35}$

5 | 10 | 9 | 7 | 10 | 2 | 100 | | 850 |

Tim: 850 $\frac{10}{35}$ Allan: 850 $\frac{10}{45}$

$(9 \times 100 = 900 \quad 7 - 2 = 5 \quad 5 \times 10 = 50 \quad 900 - 50 = 850)$

6 | G | L | A | N | D | H | I | R | E |

Tim: HERALDING $\frac{10}{45}$ Allan: *failed* $\frac{0}{45}$

7 | R | D | L | E | O | A | Y | R | I |

Tim: DREARILY $\frac{8}{53}$ Allan: DARIEL *invalid* $\frac{0}{45}$

8 | 9 | 7 | 8 | 2 | 10 | 50 | | 306 |

Tim: 306 $\frac{10}{63}$ Allan: 306 $\frac{10}{55}$

$(10 - 9 = 1 \quad 7 - 1 = 6 \times 50 = 300 \quad 8 - 2 = 6 + 300 = 306)$

9 | D | R | U | B | A | H | E | R | O |

Tim: *failed* $\frac{0}{63}$ Allan: HARBOURED $\frac{10}{65}$

10 | T | F | G | A | E | O | V | R | I |

Tim: FRIGATE $\frac{0}{63}$ Allan: FAVORITE $\frac{8}{73}$

11 | 4 | 6 | 3 | 5 | 8 | 5 | | 272 |

Tim: 274 $\frac{0}{63}$ Allan: 273 $\frac{7}{80}$

(Allan: $8 \times 5 = 40$ $4 + 3 = 7$ $6 - 5 = 1$ $40 - 1 = 39$
$39 \times 7 = 273$)

It is possible to produce 272. *See page* 167

12	F I N E D A G E N	DEAFENING	10		*failed*	0
			73			80

13	T P T H E A E C W	TEACH	5		PEACH	5
			78			85

14	3 4 8 2 7 9 852	860	5		860	5
			83			90

$(3 + 7 = 10$ $8 + 2 = 10 \times 9 = 90 - 4 = 86 \times 10 = 860)$

15	R O Y D A N C E S	*failed*	0	SECONDARY	10
			83		100

John Meade

COUNTDOWN CLASSICS – IMPROVED SOLUTIONS

Olivia Lloyd-Potts versus Darryl Francis

Round 6. $9 \times 50 = 450 + 100 = 550$ $8 + 4 + 1 = 13$
$550 - 13 = 537$

Round 11.   ACTIVE, OCTAVE and AVOCET were available for 6 points. But, CAVETTO would have scored 7 points.

Ian Bebbington versus Julian Hough

Round 10. $4 \times 25 = 100$ $7 + 8 = 15$ $(100 + 15) \times 6 = 690$

Round 13. $50 - 7 = 43$ $43 - 6 = 37$ $37 \times 25 = 925$
$10 \div 5 = 2$ $925 - 2 = 923$

Clive Spate versus Anthony Butcher

Round 1.   ALONGSIDE for 18 points.

Round 2.   CRUSTS for 6 points. But, SANCTUS for 7 points.

Round 12.   VOLUME for 6 points.

Mick Keeble versus David Trace

Round 2.   ASTEROID, TARDIEST and STRIATED were available for 8 points. Whilst 'ADROITEST' for a possible 18 points can be discerned, this would not be accepted on purely grammatical grounds.

Round 13. $100 + 75 = 175$ $5 \div 5 = 1 + 8 = 9$
$175 - 9 = 166$ $166 \times 4 = 664$

David Reid versus John Clarke

Round 8.   DANDIEST, LANDSLIDE and ISLANDED were available for 8 points. (Note that ISLAND *as a verb* will be deleted from the new edition of the *Concise*.)

Round 10. $5 + 1 = 6 \times 6 = 36 + 2 = 38 \times 25 = 950 - 4 = 946$

Kevin Nelson versus Hilary Hopper

Round 1.   FRUITION for 8 points.

Round 4.   APNOEA or PHENOL for 6 points.

Round 6. $50 + 5 = 55$ $8 + 6 = 14$ $55 \times 14 = 770 - 4 = 766$

Round 9.   SERAPHIM or SAMPHIRE for 8 points.

Round 11.   BRAWNIER for 8 points.

Roger Wales versus Tony Vick
Round 4.   NATIVE or VOTIVE for 6 points.
Round 6. $50 + 7 = 57 - 1 = 56$ $9 + 1 = 10$
   $56 \times 10 = 560 - 4 = 556$
Round 9.   FAZING or EFFING for 6 points.

Mark Nyman versus Joyce Cansfield
Round 4. $75 + 7 = 82 \times 8 = 656 - 10 = 646$

Clive Freedman versus Peter Evans
Round 3. $5 \times 6 = 30 - 8 = 22 \times 25 = 550$ $8 + 3 = 11$
   $550 - 11 = 539$
Round 8.   EPINASTY for 8 points.
Round 10. $75 - 10 = 65 \times 6 = 390$ $9 + 3 = 12$
   $390 + 12 = 402$
Round 13. $4 \times 50 = 200 + 9 = 209 \times 4 = 836$
   $5 \div 5 = 1 + 836 = 837$

Tim Morrissey versus Allan Saldanha
Round 11. $8 \times 5 = 40$ $4 + 3 = 7$ $6 - 1 = 5$
   $40 - 1 = 39 \times 7 = 273$

Glossary

The prime or, in most cases, the unique sources for the words which constitute the acceptable AEGINRST transposals are:

Oxford English Dictionary, Webster's 1st, 2nd and 3rd International Dictionaries, Funk & Wagnalls New Standard Dictionary (1972 edition), English Dialect Dictionary, Chambers Scots Dictionary, Gould's Medical Dictionary, Musical Instruments — a Comprehensive Dictionary, Webster's Biographical Dictionary, Columbia Lippincott Gazetteer of the World, Times-Index Gazetteer of the World and A Hammond Ambassador World Atlas.

In the specific case of the word TIGREANS, the acceptance of this pluralized noun is not that of a language uniquely mentioned in Webster's 2nd (and Borgmann's quoted authority for inclusion in the AEGINRST listing) but as the sensible plural of a TIGREAN person. This particular citation occurred in a December 1987 issue of Time magazine after the death of Borgmann and after the publication of Pears Advanced Word-Puzzler's Dictionary.

Whilst TIGREANS is now on file for any future editions of the Pears Advanced Word-Puzzler's Dictionary, the singular in the sense of a person does not occur in any known dictionary, so that it has yet to be 'legitimized' for any word game which permits words in the upper case. All of the 'missing' anagrams are also held on the Pears Advanced Word-Puzzler's Dictionary's files for this purpose of future inclusion.

The remaining words defined in the Glossary will normally be found in at least two dictionaries. Therefore, only the AEGINRST anagrams will carry references to prime sources and individual footnotes such as (OED/PAW-PD) which means that the essential authority is the *Oxford English Dictionary* and that *Pears Advanced Word-Puzzler's Dictionary* also carries the word. By contrast, a note such as (EDD) means that the word can be found or inferred from an entry in the *English Dialect Dictionary* and the anagram is unique to the Borgmann collection. The abbreviations used for these works are included in the general listing below.

ABBREVIATIONS

adj	adjective
adv	adverb
arch	archaic
CLG	*Columbia Lippincott Gazetteer*
collq	colloquial
comp	comparative
CSD	*Chambers Scots Dictionary*
dial	dialect – a dialect of England unless otherwise specified
EDD	*English Dialect Dictionary*
erron	erroneous
fm	form (of)
FW	Funk & Wagnalls
GMD	*Gould's Medical Dictionary*
HAA	*Hammond Ambassador Atlas*
interj	interjection
Ir	Irish (specifically Irish English)
MID	*Musical Instruments Dictionary*
n	noun
now	formerly standard English now found only as designated (i.e. *now* S now only Literary Scottish)
Obs	obsolete *before* 1500
obs	obsolete *after* 1500
OED	*Oxford English Dictionary*
pa pple	past participle
PAW-PD	*Pears Advanced Word-Puzzler's Dictionary*
pers n	personal name
pl	plural
qv	denotes a cross reference to
S	Scottish (specifically Literary Scottish, an independent English language, unless qualified as given below)

S & *dial*	Literary Scottish and a dialect or dialects of England
S *dial*	a Scottish dialect, not Literary Scottish
TIG	*Times-Index Gazetteer*
var fm	a variant form of
vb	verb
W1	*Webster's International Dictionary* (first edition)
W2	*Webster's* second edition
W3	*Webster's* third edition
WBD	*Webster's Biographical Dictionary*

aa *n* a cooled cindery substance consisting of sand, earth, stones and melted lava

adz *n* an ax-like tool with the blade set at right angles. (Note that dictionaries are at odds with each other over **adz** and **adze**. The OED has **adz** as the basic form for the noun, with **adze** as an alternative spelling. For the verb (to use this tool) it gives the form **adze** only. The *Concise* has **adze** as the basic form for both the noun and verb with **adz** as a 'chiefly USA' form for the noun and verb. *Chambers* carries no mention of the verb and gives only **adze**. The American *Official Scrabble Players Dictionary* has **adz** as the basic form with **adze** as the alternative and, again, carries no mention of the verb. *Funk & Wagnalls Standard* has **adze** as the basic form for both noun and verb with **adz** as an international alternative. *Collins Concise* has **adze** as the basic, with **adz** as the US form. This is for the noun only, it carries no mention of the verb. From the standpoint of games players, this means that **adz**, **adze**, **adzes**, **adzed** and **adzing** are all valid for *Countdown*. For Scrabble in the UK only **adze** and **adzes** are valid. For Scrabble in the USA, Canada, Australia, the West Indies, Israel etc. **adz**, **adze** and **adzes** are valid. For all other games it will depend entirely upon which dictionary you consult)

aflaj see **falaj**

agouti *n* a rabbit-sized American rodent (*pl* **agoutis**/**agouties** of which only the former may be presumed for *Countdown*, as neither is specifically given in the *Concise*)

ambivert *n* one who is intermediate between an introvert and an extrovert

alpe *var fm n* **alp** in the specific sense as a bullfinch

ambulant *adj* meanings include moving about from place to place

ana *n* a collection of a person's memorable sayings

andolandol *n* a Chinese fly, a tincture of which is used as a blistering agent

angelus *n* a series of prayers recited in the R.C. Church thrice daily (Note that the word appears in the lower case in the *Concise* and both of the Scrabble reference works, thus validating it for word games. It appears in the upper case in *Collins Concise*, whereas *Funk & Wagnalls* gives a choice of forms)

angrite *n* a meteoritic stone consisting essentially of titanaugite and having no chondrules (rounded granules) embedded in it (W3/PAW-PD)

ankh *n* a keylike cross, the ancient Egyptian symbol for life

anserine *adj* of or like a goose: silly

anther *n* the pollen-bearing part of a plant's stamen

areg see **erg**

arest *obs fm n/vb* **arrest** (OED/PAW-PD)

astringe *vb* to constrict, compress, bind together (OED/W3/PAW-PD)

axillae *pl* **axilla**, the armpit

azelea *n* a shrubby plant cultivated for its showy pink or purple flowers

azimuth *n* its meanings include the horizontal angle of a bearing clockwise from north

bezique *n* a particular card game (Note that pluralized, it is one of the two highest-scoring 8-letter words available for either UK or US championship Scrabble, providing that it is correctly positioned on a peripheral line)

blooper *colloq n* an error

caballero *n* Spanish gentleman

calcite *n* a mineral, of which the transparent variety is known as **Iceland spar**

cangue *n* a large heavy wooden block which, in the China of an earlier time, was fixed around the neck of a convicted person who, though mobile, could no longer use his arms to feed himself and needed to rely upon the charity of others. Such a criminal was undergoing 'the punishment of the cha'

cannelure *n* a groove

caprine *adj* goatlike

carotene *n* an orange or red substance formed in such as carrots

cavetto *n* a type of architectural hollow moulding (*pl* **cavetti** and, not available for *Countdown*, **cavettos**)

clavier *n* meanings include a keyboard

clerihew *n* a four-line versified witty, comic or nonsensical biography invented by Edmund *Clerihew* Bentley (1875–1956). His master-pieces include:

> The digestion of Milton
> Was unequal to Stilton.
> He was only feeling so-so
> When he wrote Il *Penseroso*.

cloacinal *nonce adj* pertaining to, or characterized by, a cloaca (The standard *adj* with this meaning is **cloacal** and *Chambers* also carries **cloacaline** which is another *nonce adj* with the same meaning. It also has an alternative spelling for cloacaline which dispenses with the E and which appears to be exclusive to that particular dictionary. Ironically, the anagram of CLOACINAL/CLOACALIN is LACONICAL, an obsolete *adj* which *Chambers* gives as extant!)

coralline *adj* of the nature of, like or resembling coral: red (i.e. the colour of red coral) *n* a seaweed of the genus *Corallina*

coypu *n* a large aquatic rodent native to South America but which is now found wild all over the world. Apart from the USSR, where they were deliberately released, these emigrants are descended from escapees from fur farms. Its only close relative is the hutia of the West Indies

cranet *obs n* a piece of armour for the back of a horse's neck *obs dial n* a little red worm

creant *adj* creative

curtilage *n* now essentially only a legal term for the land which comprises the total – including that covered by buildings – associated with a residence (in the southwest of England a *var fm*, **courtledge**, is still in general usage)

cwm *n* a natural amphitheatre caused by glacial erosion *Welsh n* a (deep) narrow valley

dariole *n* a dish cooked and served in a small mould

displode *vb* to discharge with explosive violence: to explode (Both the OED and W2 record the *vb* as *obs* though it is also carried by the OSPD which has no distinctive labels)

diuretic *n* that which increases the flow of urine (also *adj*)

dryad *n* a wood nymph of classical myth: a beautiful maiden who lives in a forest: a tree (Note that of its two plural *fms* only **dryads** may be presumed for *Countdown*, whereas **dryades** is also available for Scrabble on either side of the Atlantic)

duenna *n* in such as Spain or Portugal, an elderly woman who acts as a governess-cum-chaperone to the girl or girls of a family

eclogue *n* a pastoral poem usually in the form of a conversation

ee S *n* an eye (Interestingly, this is one of those rare words, discussed elsewhere, which still retain a Middle English plural form. In this case it is **een**)

egger *n* any of various species of moths which, at one stage in their existence, live in an egg-shaped cocoon. Its *var fm* is **eggar**

epiblast *n* meanings include the outermost germ layer of the embryo

epinasty *n* (downward curvature of a plant's organ induced by) a more active growth on its upper side

epopt *n* one initiated into the ancient Greek Eleusinian mysteries

erg *n* area of shifting sand dunes in the Sahara (*pl* **ergs** or **areg**)

erigant *erron fm obs n* **herigaut**, a cloak worn by either sex in the 13th/14th centuries (OED/PAW-PD. Both Borgmann and the PAW-PD are skating on thin ice by accepting a plural for what is essentially a Middle English word. Herigaut, spelt in various ways, had a life-span from 1297 to 1727 in recorded literature and it is unclear as to the exact period when erigant would have been used. The fact that it is an erroneous form does not invalidate the word from a game player's standpoint but the plural is suspect)

eyebright *n* a plant with small white-and-purple flowers formerly used as a remedy for weak eyesight

falaj *n Chambers* defines this as 'a water channel specif. one forming part of the irrigation system of Oman' and provides the plural, **aflaj**

fite S *dial var fm adj/n/vb* **white** (Note that this particular spelling form occurs only in the dialect of Banff though, in Kentish dialect, the form **fyte** is an English equivalent)

fitz *n* a son (An Anglo-French word originally used as a standard term, it is now found only in surnames e.g. Fitzgerald, Fitzherbert etc. though Lord Macaulay used **Fitz** as a nonce word describing people with such surnames. A 13th-century spelling as FYZ scores 5.1 on the Sumwords scale)

forestay *n* a stay which supports a ship's foremast

gainter *var fm dial vb* **gander**, to wander, ramble aimlessly (EDD)

'gairnest' Borgmann's presumption of a poetic second person singular present active indicative form of the *vb* **gairn**, a Northumberland *var fm* of **girn** (qv) (EDD)

gairten S *fm n* **garter** (W3. Though overlooked by PAW-PD, it does carry a similar S *fm*, **garten**, which features in a different anagram listing – how STRANGE!)

gaitner *dial n* one who binds grain into sheaves (FW)

Galangalan *n* a mountain in Sorsogon Province, Luzon Island, the Philippines

galipot *n* the turpentine or resin which exudes from and hardens upon certain pines (the plural allowed on *Countdown* is grammatically suspect)

ganderism *nonce n* conduct befitting a gander

gasterin *n* a preparation of the gastric juices of dogs, used as a pepsin (GMD)

gastrine *var fm n* **gastrin**, a hormone made in the pyloric glands of the stomach (GMD)

genitras *obs n pl* testicles (OED under **genitor**)

Ginestar a town in the province of Tarragona in northeastern Spain (CL)

girn *now S, Ir & dial vb* to show teeth in rage, pain or disappointment: to snarl as a dog: to complain persistently: to be fretful or peevish: to show teeth in laughing: to grin (Note: GIRNING MATCH This celebrated rustic sport, essentially local to Westmoreland, has the participants in competition as to who can produce the ugliest grin whilst his face is framed by a horse's collar. The most famous exponent of this activity is the comedian Les Dawson who, on TV, regularly displays a typical girning action with his delightfully inane grin which has his nose and chin coming much closer together)

gnast *obs vb* to gnash (Note: The only recorded spelling *fm* of

gnaster is **gnastere** c 1440 which is Borgmann's evidence for the potential of his 'gnaister'. (OED))

grantise *Obs n* permission, consent, grant (OED/PAW-PD)

Gretian *obs fm n/adj* **Grecian** (OED/PAW-PD)

grommet *n* a ring of such as rubber designed to line a hole to prevent chafing of that passing through

gymp *var fm n* **gimp** in the sense of silk, worsted or cotton yarn with a hard core of cord or wire used for such as trimming

halliard *var fm n* **halyard**, a nautical term for a rope used for raising or lowering such as a sail or a flag

hetaira *n* a courtesan (*pl* **hetairas**, **hetairai**)

hoatzin *n* the stink bird, a very primitive South American species of bird which resembles a smelly, clumsy, underfed and particularly untidy chicken. Its young possess claws on their wings which they use for tree climbing

iambi *pl* **iambus**, a term in prosody for a metric foot consisting of one short followed by one long syllable. The alternative *pl* is **iambuses**

ide *n* the orfe, a European carp-like fish

igerant *var fm dial n* **ignorant**, an ignorant person – ironically, this spelling form exists only in the dialect of Oxford! (EDD)

incubi *pl* **incubus**, a male demon supposed to have sex with a sleeping woman as opposed to a **succubus** which invades a sleeping man for a similar purpose. The alternative *pl* is **incubuses**

ingestar *obs n* an Italian early 17th-century wine bottle (OED/PAW-PD)

ingreat *obs vb* to magnify or make great (OED/PAW-PD)

inlier *n* an outcrop of rock encased in rock of a later formation

introitus *n* the entrance to the vagina

ismatic *nonce adj* pertaining to an ism or isms *nonce n* one who belongs to a particular ism (*Chambers* also carries the equally nonce *adj* **ismatical** which again, it gives as standard!)

isochime *var fm n* **isocheim**, a line on a map connecting places with the same average winter temperature (Note that this *var fm* does not appear in the *Concise* so it is invalid for the television version of *Countdown*. It does appear, however, in such as *Collins Concise* and *Chambers* so that it is acceptable for the boxed version of the game. As either *fm* is a trivial anagram of the other so nothing is lost for the television version)

kibbutz *n* a communal farming settlement in modern Israel (*pl* **kibbutzim**)

kohlrabi *n* a variety of cabbage with a turnip-shaped stem

lacerant *nonce adj* of a sound, harrowing

lacertine *adj* pertaining to lizards: of an ornament, consisting of intertwined figures of lizards

lagniappe *n* a thing given as a bonus or gratuity

lapilli *n pl* fragments of lava ejected from a volcano (Note that the singular, **lapillus**, does not appear in either the *Concise* or *Chambers* and is thus unavailable for television *Countdown* and UK Scrabble. Given in such as *Collins Concise* the singular is valid for the boxed version of *Countdown* and is also available for Scrabble outside the UK. As Waddington's games bar plurals, so you have a real problem on your hands sorting out validity for such as Lexicon)

lepa *n* the fragments which adhere to the hands of the one who offers a ball of rice to deceased ancestors in a Hindu ceremony

lionet *n* a small or young lion

lorimer *n* one who makes (especially for a horse's harness) small metal items

macaw *n* any of fifteen species of large, intelligent parrots with brilliant (usually multicoloured) plumage: a species of palm tree

manward *arch adj* tending or directed towards man

matzo *n* a wafer of unleavened bread (*pl* **matzos**, **matzoth**)

mewl *vb* cry feebly, whimper, mew like a cat

modester *comp adj* modest (Note that whilst specifically given in the Scrabble reference works and tolerated on a particular edition of *Countdown*, it is only marginally satisfactory. However, the OED does carry a quote of 1591 which justifies acceptance. In this example it speaks of a woman who was 'not the *modestest* wife in the world')

moider *dial vb* to perplex, confuse, worry

murex *n* any of various species of carnivorous molluscs including the Venus comb (*pl* **murices**, **murexes**)

muscarine *n* a poison found in certain fungi

'nargiest' This is Borgmann's supposition that the *adj* NARGIE (meaning jeering) is capable of taking a superlative form. NARGIE appears to be exclusive to CSD as neither the *Scottish National Dictionary* nor the EDD carry it, though the latter does have NYARGIE (!) with the same sense of jeering. To infer that something is capable of being the 'most jeering' is akin to implying that one would describe that something as the 'jeeringest' of all. Would you use such a term?!

negarit *var fm n* **nagarit**, one of a pair of Ethiopian kettledrums (MID)

negrita *n* the *Hypoplectrus chlorurus*, a violet-black coloured fish with yellow fins found in the waters of the West Indies and Florida (FW)

netsuke *n* a Japanese carved toggle of either wood or ivory used for suspending articles from a sash around the waist

Ngotangota *n* a town on the western shore of Lake Malawi

niello *n* a black compound of sulphur and such as silver or lead used to incise a design on a metal surface: the process: that so decorated (*pl* **nielli**, **niellos**)

noetic *adj* of or pertaining to the mind *n* (also in the *fm* **noetics**) the science of the intellect (Note that whilst **noetics** is available for *Countdown*, it is invalid for Scrabble either side of the Atlantic as their reference works carry the *adj* only)

nonage *n* meanings include any age of immaturity

nonce word a word coined by a writer, often very eminent, for a particular (usually unique) occasion and which word has not become part of normal usage. A typical example is Ben Jonson's **un-in-one-breath-utterable**

orang *n* the **orang-utan** (also known as **orangutang** and **urangutang**) a manlike large ape of the forests of Borneo and Sumatra with strong arms and shaggy reddish-brown hair

ortolan *n* any of several birds especially a European bunting highly esteemed as a table delicacy

oxidize *vb* meanings include to undergo a chemical reaction with oxygen (Note that Waddington's plural rules technically render such as **oxidizes** valid and **oxen** invalid – which is probably not what they intended for their games! *Countdown* has no such legalistic ambiguities)

padle S *n* the lumpfish, a clumsy sea fish: a hoe or similar scraping implement

palp *vb* to touch, feel

paple S *fm vb* **popple**, to bubble

papple S *fm vb* **popple**, to bubble

parodist *n* the author of a parody

pela *n* China wax, a white wax obtained from an insect

pepperpot *n* a pepperbox or (small) container with a perforated lid used for sprinkling pepper: a West Indian stew of meat or fish with okra, chilies and other vegetables: in Pennsylvania, a soup of tripe and dough balls highly seasoned with pepper (Note: Whilst the *Concise* has **pepper-pot** it does not hyphenate **pepperbox** and the unhyphenated **pepperpot** is given in such highly respected works as *Funk & Wagnalls Standard Dictionary* as well as appearing in one of the quotes in the *Oxford English Dictionary*. By contrast, both the *Oxford American Dictionary* and *Collins Concise* prefer to treat it as two separate words, **pepper pot**. Which is correct? All three forms are perfectly acceptable, but the games player must respect whichever form is given in the particular dictionary used for arbitration in the event of a dispute. Hence the word is invalid for *Countdown* and Shelling Peas unless players of Maxwell Caulfield's game happen to possess a dictionary which agrees with his carefully researched verdict)

peto *n* the wahoo, a dark-blue edible fish

phonate *vb* to utter vocal sound

phut *n* a dull sound of impact

pia *n* a species of tropical plant, cultivated for its tubers which are the source of Tahiti arrowroot

pinnace *n* any of various types of small boat attached to a ship

plap *vb* to fall with a flat impact

polenta *n* a porridge made of maize meal etc.

pote *n* a stick or rod used for poking

pronate *vb* meanings include to turn the palm downwards

proteid *n* a protein: a species of salamander

pshaw *interj* expressing contempt or impatience

pteropid *adj* belonging to or having the characteristics of the flying fox family

purslane *n* a fleshy leaved herb formerly used in salads

pya *n* a species of plant, the tubers of which supply arrowroot

Q, q as an independent word in its own right it was used as late as the 17th century as an alternative spelling for **cue** in various meanings. One of the more interesting of these is given below under the heading **qu**

qu *obs n* a notional sum of half-a-farthing used in bookkeeping. Technically, it is a *var fm* of **cue** and was also written as **Q** or **q**. The actual half-farthing occurred subsequently. The plural for this delightful word is either **qus** (as recorded in 1597) or **ques** (1674) and players of various crossword-type games treasure this little coin

quixotize *vb* to act in an absurdly generous and extravagantly chivalrous manner

qw- Apart from being an alternative form of QU- and still retained in dialect as such, it was also an earlier alternative for words commencing CH- and WH-. Examples:

    QU- **qwest** (quest): **qwykn** (quicken)
    CH- **qweer** (choir): **qwere** (choir)
    WH- **qwhyt** (white): **qwi**   (why)

The revival of QWAINT (quaint) has this modern noun with both its current and obsolete adjectival meanings. Chaucer's bawdy noun QUAINT never had the QW- spelling form

qwat *dial vb* to squash flat

qwerty *adj* designating the standard arrangement of keys on a typewriter keyboard (Note: *Chambers* also has it as a noun and its *Official Scrabble Words* provides both 'qwerties' and 'qwertys' as acceptable plural forms)

qwine *dial n* money: a corner

qwirk *var fm dial n* **quirk**, a twist, a bend (The QW- form does not apply to the *dial vb* **quirk**, to grunt: to grumble)

qwop *dial vb* to throb with pain

qwot *var fm dial vb* **qwat** (qv)

ragstone *n* meanings include any of various kinds of hard, coarse stone which break up into flat pieces several inches thick

raing S *dial vb* to encircle

rangaranga *n* the local name in the Caroline Islands for parsley fern growing in the cracks of walls

rantipole *adj* wild and reckless *n* such a person (Note that the *vb*, to behave in such a fashion, is not given in the *Concise*. From a

Countdown standpoint this is immaterial as it is already a word of maximum length, but a Scrabble player can convert such as RAN, ANT or TIP into (say) RANTIPOLED by the addition of seven tiles for a bonus score)

ratherest *adv* most of all, most particularly (*now dial* except in the phrase *rather of the ratherest*, just a touch too much or, conversely, just a touch too little)

ravelin *n* an historical defensive outwork having two faces forming a salient angle

reast *var fm now dial vb* **reest**, to become rancid (OED/PAW-PD)

Registan an extensive sandy desert region in southernmost Afghanistan (HAWA)

renigat *obs* S *fm now dial n* **renegate**, a deserter (OED/PAW-PD)

Restinga an African town on the northernmost coast of Morocco (TIG)

rhyolite *n* a fine-grained igneous rock

routinist *n* one governed by self-imposed routine

salient *adj/n* meanings include (that which) is conspicuous or prominent

Scotian *obs nonce adj* of or belonging to Scotland

sergiant *obs fm n* **sergeant** (OED/PAW-PD)

sestertia *pl* **sestertium**, the sum of a thousand sesterces (a sesterce being an old Roman coin of varying value)

shofroth *pl* **shofar**, an ancient Hebrew musical instrument made from a ram's horn

soutane *n* cassock of R.C. priest

stear *obs fm vb* **steer**, to guide (OED/PAW-PD)

stimuli *pl* **stimulus**, a goad

stingaree *n* either of the two species of the largest of the stingrays, the *Dasyatis brevicaudata*, first sighted by Captain Cook in Australasian waters, or the *Dasyatis centroura* of the western North Atlantic. The term began as a casual word in US and Australian speech for any species of stingray and it is in this sense that the word is defined in the *Concise*. However, as a standard term in English, scientific writers use it only for the species named above

straigne *obs fm vb* **strain** (OED/PAW-PD)

strainge *obs fm adj* **strange** (OED/PAW-PD)

strangie *var fm obs adj* **strangy**, strange (OED)

succinate *n* a salt of succinic acid (an acid obtained from amber and formerly known as **spirit of amber**)

syzygy *n* meanings include the positioning of a celestial body (such as the moon) in a direct line with the earth and the sun. Which body is then said to be *at* syzygy

Tangiers the well known Moroccan seaport (Note: Apart from giving this sensible word, Borgmann claims another AEGINRST 'anagram' with TANGIER'S – a plural of the comparative adjective! This gives you some idea as to how the total of 150 has been compiled)

tanistry *n* the ancient Irish system of life-tenure given, by election, to the 'eldest and worthiest' of the surviving menfolk of a lord

tanrec *var fm n* **tenrec**, any one of a number of different species of insectivores akin to the moles and shrews, though many resemble hedgehogs. They vary in adult size from that of a rabbit to that of a mouse and their activities, according to species, are similar to hedgehogs, moles or otters

tarieng *obs fm n* **tarrying** (OED)

tearing *n* an abnormal watering of the eyes for *various* physical reasons (W3/PAW-PD. In accepting a plural, the games player has the significant word *various* to justify such a reasonable assumption)

tetragon *n* a four-sided figure

thalweg *n* a line where opposite geological slopes meet: such a line, as the centre of a river, used as a legal boundary

ti *n* a tree or shrub of the genus *Cordyline* especially C. *terminalis* with edible roots

Tigranes *pers n* the name of several kings of ancient Armenia, most notably Tigranes the Great who reigned from 95 BC to 55 BC (WBD)

Tigrean *n* a Semitic language and one of a people in northern Ethiopia (see introduction to Glossary)

torque *n* meanings include a necklace of twisted metal

trapes *collq vb* to walk in a trailing or untidy way (Note: The *Concise* has this as a *var fm vb* **traipse** whereas the OED gives **trapes** as the basic form. The OED gives, in addition, both TRAPESING and TRAIPSING as nouns, quoting Thomas Hardy as using the latter spelling form)

travois *n* a Red Indian primitive sled based on two poles attached to a draught animal and dragged behind it (*pl* **travois** or, but not available for *Countdown*, **travoises**)

trefoil *n* meanings include any plant of the clover family

udal *n* a kind of freehold right once common in Northern Europe before the feudal system and still extant in Orkney and Shetland

uraemia *n* the accumulation in the blood of waste products normally expelled in urine

urangutang/orangutang *var fms n* **orang-utan** (see **orang**)

valance *n* a short piece of suspended drapery on such as a bed

vesicate *vb* to raise blisters on

virago *n* a loud, violent or ill-tempered woman (*pl* **viragos/viragoes** of which only the former is valid for *Countdown*)

virelay *n* an old French short lyric poem (rare in English) with two rhymes to a stanza variously repeated

vortices *pl* **vortex**, a whirling mass of such as liquid, gas or flame

wahine *n* a Maori woman

wynd *n* a narrow street or passage turning off from a main thoroughfare: a lane or alley (Whilst usage is mainly confined to Scotland and northern England it is a standard English word and writers have used it for similar passageways in such as Paris)

xebec *n* a type of small Mediterranean sailing vessel

xenophobe *n* a person with a morbid dislike of foreigners

xylem *n* wood as a tissue of the body of the higher plants – its functions include conducting water and mineral salts from the roots to all other parts

yataghan *n* a Turkish curved (double edged) sword or scimitar without a guard (Note that the *var fms* **yatagan** and **atagan** do not occur in the *Concise* and that *Chambers* appears to be unique in describing this weapon as a dagger)

yblent *arch adj* blended

yclept *pa pple arch vb* **clepe**, to call: to name. Hence, used adjectively to mean called, named or styled

yibbles *Chambers* defines this as a Scottish adverb meaning 'perhaps'. It would appear to be exclusive to that work. The PAW-PD has **yibble** as a *var fm dial vb* **yivel**, to make a crooked furrow in ploughing

ywroken *arch adj* punished, avenged

yucca *n* the state flower of New Mexico: any of a large genus of liliaceous plants having a short woody stem which bears a mass of these white bell-shaped flowers

zephyr *n* meanings include a soft, gentle breeze

zetetic *adj* proceeding by inquiry (Note that the rare *n* – meanings include inquiry – is valid for UK Scrabble but not *Countdown*. Neither **zetetic** nor **zetetics** is valid for USA Scrabble

zeugma *n* a figure of speech in which an adjective modifies or a verb governs two or more words although appropriate to only one of them or making a different sense with each e.g.

> He took his hat and his leave. or She was remembered but they forgotten.

zeugmatic *adj* pertaining to or involving zeugma

zinco *n* a zincograph or etched zinc plate used in printing: a print therefrom (*pl* **zincos**) *vb* to etch on zinc: to print from a zincograph

zircon *n* a variously coloured gemstone

zy *Obs fm of* **the**

zygal *adj* H-shaped

zzz see **zzzz**

zzzz *n* a snore *vb* to snore (Note that a multiplicity of Zs in varying lengths can be found in the OED's quotes, all of which express the sound of snoring or buzzing. Four Zs appears to be the most popular literary form, though three Zs is a fair alternative. The OED had noted the use of ZZZZ by H. G. Wells (1909) and the *New Yorker* (1975) and, of course, it also appears in the *American Thesaurus of Slang*. ZZZ occurred as a verb in the internationally syndicated *Peanuts* strip cartoon on the back page of the *Daily Mail*, 12 June 1989 as well as having word player's legitimacy by being noted in the *Hamlyn* dictionary. From a game player's standpoint, only ZZZ and ZZZZ may be considered as valid words, even though usage of Zs in excess of four can be found in the OED's quotations. This is because only ZZZ and ZZZZ have occurred as headwords in a dictionary and, therefore, brought themselves within the scope of use.

Peter Newby

Countdown *Honours* List

CHAMPIONSHIP OF CHAMPIONS FINAL SCORES

Series 5	Mark Nyman (Played over 9 rounds only)	65 points
Series 9	Clive Freedman	91 points
Series 13	Harvey Freeman	115 points
Series 13	Nic Brown	78 points

COUNTDOWN CHAMPIONS

Series 1	Joyce Cansfield
Series 2	Ash Haji
Series 3	Brian Hudson
Series 4	Andrew Guy
Series 5	Peter Evans
Series 6	Darryl Francis
Series 7	Ian Bebbington
Series 8	Clive Spate
Series 9	David Trace

Series 10	Harvey Freeman
Series 11	John Clarke
Series 12	Stephen Balment
Series 13	Hilary Hopper
Series 14	Nic Brown
Series 15	Dick Green
Series 16	Tony Vick
Series 17	Lawrence Pearse
Series 18	Dr Rajaretnam Yogasaganar

HIGHEST SCORES IN NORMAL GAME

Series 13	Mike Whiteoak	80 points
Series 15	Allan Saldanha (age 10 years)	81 points
Series 10	Harvey Freeman	82 points
Series 12	Stephen Balment	83 points
Series 18	Jonathan Anstey	81 points

HIGHEST SCORES IN FINAL

Series 14	Nic Brown	108 points
Series 8	Clive Spate	107 points
Series 16	Tony Vick	100 points

Acknowledgements

The supreme anagram is fully detailed in four issues of the magazine, Word Ways. These are the August and November 1976, the February 1977 and the November 1979 issues, all of which are available on microfilm from University Microfilms (A Bell and Howell Company), 300 North Zeeb Road, Ann Arbor, MI 48106, USA.

Founded by Dmitri Borgmann in 1968, Word Ways consists of many and various articles on the subject of words and the majority of its writers are established authors, including its current editor and publisher. A. Ross Eckler. A quarterly magazine, it is available in the U.K. only on direct annual subscription of $17 including postage, though some back issues may be purchased individually. Anyone wishing for further information on any Word Ways subject discussed in this book should contact the publisher and editor at Word Ways, Spring Valley Road, Morristown, New Jersey 07960, USA.

Plod the Salmon occurs in a Thompsonnet in the preface to Fly Fishing by J. R. Hartley (published by Yell Opages). This was written in gratitude for all the kind attention she gave to the technical detail, so vital to the book.